THE GARDEN

THE GARDEN
A YEAR AT HOME FARM
DAN PEARSON
PHOTOGRAPHY BY NICOLA BROWNE

EBURY PRESS
LONDON

PRELUDE

This is a story about a dream, a place and how we came to understand the sensibility of the place. It is also about a great friendship rooted in common ideals. Most of all, it is about realizing that whichever way man turns, nature has its own way of making us very humble. **Frances Mossman**

Home Farm has taught us many things. We have learnt not to be afraid of change or of moving forward. We have learnt to be flexible and not to be sentimental, and that mistakes are often the most thought-provoking and interesting happenings on the journey. The garden has been about a development of ideas and confidence and I have to thank my dear friend Frances for encouraging that and making it all possible. **Dan Pearson**

CONTENTS

HISTORY

Frances and I were introduced in 1983. She had been teaching fashion at Winchester College of Art with my mother and they had fallen into conversation about Frances' new garden in London. I was studying horticulture at Wisley at the time and when Frances said that she was looking for help with her garden, my mother suggested we should meet.

One day in June Frances picked me up after work and we travelled down to Hampshire to see the garden I had created at my parents' home. We talked about plants all the way there and all the way back. Both passionate about Beth Chatto's stand at the Chelsea Flower Show, we discovered that we shared an aesthetic. Frances also talked about her need to move her garden forward. She had reached a point of frustration with it. Although she could visualize the changes she wanted, she felt that she lacked the experience to make those ideas work on the ground.

That September I spent a month building her garden in Barnes with a friend from Wisley and, when I returned from a year working at the Botanical Gardens in Edinburgh, I continued to maintain it while I was studying at Kew.

To be trusted at seventeen with designing a whole garden was an incredible opportunity and Frances allowed me ample room to experiment. She has done so ever since and has never failed to give me unwavering encouragement. We work together in conversation, each time we meet, taking a walk into the garden to discuss ideas. The conversation is always hugely enriching – we talk about texture and colour and the 'feel' and mood of the garden. We bring to the table things that we have both seen or experienced elsewhere that are relevant to the place. We discuss the things which work and plan change for those that don't. There is always a project on the horizon which will be mulled over until we are confident that it is right for the place. The experience of making gardens together is all the better for collaboration, two different perspectives contributing to a whole.

I was initially horrified at the announcement that, three years after making the Barnes garden, Frances and her husband were moving. However, I was also pleased that the move was triggered by a desire to garden on a bigger scale. I had started to travel myself during this period, first to the mountains of northern Europe and then to the Himalayas and Israel, to look at the way in which plants grew together in nature. This became something of an obsession and it changed my ideas about the way in which plants could be used in gardens. I wrote long and detailed letters to Frances about what I had seen and how I wanted to garden on the side of nature, taking it as the lead, but doing so with the freedom of experimentation. We felt the same way about the new move forward.

While looking for appropriate land, the house and garden in Barnes were sold up and Frances moved into a small garden flat in north London. The best plants were boxed up and replanted into the tiny garden in a day.

This garden was the beginning of something new; it had a freedom to it that saw it balloon out in a great eruption of informality. It marked a new style that was freer and less restrictive.

We had begun to look at plants for the mood that they projected and how they could live in association with their partners rather than for their individual horticultural identity.

In 1987 we drove up to Northamptonshire to look at the four acres and derelict buildings that were to become the new home and garden. The land and aspect were perfect but it presented us with a tremendous challenge. They would give us the room to garden on the side of nature and in an environment that had a strong sense of place. We would have to garden here with a sensitive hand but a bold one.

That autumn we set about learning the new language of this place and in so doing, created the garden that now surrounds Home Farm.

GENIUS LOCI

It was high summer in 1987 when I first saw Home Farm. Frances had driven me up to Northamptonshire from London on a hot Saturday afternoon. We came off the motorway and very quickly cut into rolling farmland with thick hedgerows and overgrown verges. Before long we had rattled down the track to the old farm gate that marked the entrance to the property.

The grasses in the disused paddock at the front of the house were tall and wind tossed. Rank nettles and thistles cast dark shadows in the grass and brambles skirted the base of all the buildings. The hedgerows had grown out and were bulging with elder but they were full with the chatter of birds and the drone of bees. What was most startling was the apparent sense of isolation. The land rolled on into the distance to gently curving horizons, unmarked by buildings. All you could hear was the rustle of the wind and the insistent murmur of life in the trees.

The buildings were all but derelict. Where the walls were standing, their orange ironstone was covered in a rich patina of lichens that marked their age. The small cottage on the end of the farmhouse was on the point of falling down. The ceilings inside were hanging cracked and heavy and the walls streaked with mould where the rain had been coursing through from holes in the roof. There were rats in there. A plank nailed across the door prevented us from entering.

The tenants had been living in the third of the house that was still habitable, but beyond that the rooms were rotting and disused. There was the distant sound of running water in the cellar and the steps descending into it sank away into eight feet of water. But despite the smell of rot and the undergrowth pressing against the windows, it was immediately obvious that this was a good place; it carried no sinister overtones.

The land at the rear of the property pushed down on the extension, a narrow bramble-infested gulley being all that separated the bank from the rear walls. There was evidence of an old vegetable garden up in the far reaches of this area but brambles, thistles and bindweed had long since taken over. There was a stillness here.

The barn in 1987.

The front of the house in 1987 with its Victorian railings, before the new dry-stone wall was constructed.

The rear of the house, autumn 1987, just after the land was
first cleared of undergrowth.

Frances with her son, Tom.

The outlying buildings lay in an advanced state of decay. The bottom half of the barn had crumbled away where the gutters had corroded and the yard at the back was eight feet high with nettles, which we later discovered were growing in a vast manure heap that had filled the enclosure. The milking parlours had fallen in on themselves and the gates had fallen off their hinges; the whole place was heavy with neglect.

We sat on the small bank in front of the house in the sunshine and watched the seed separating itself from the great swathes of creeping thistle and blowing across the land at the front. The stone path and the walls were hot from the day's sunshine. There was magic in this place. It had an atmosphere all of its own.

It was this sense of place that we needed to protect. Any mark made on the land would have to be made with a sensitive hand to maintain the mood here. The walls and the land spoke for themselves, and as we reflected on the tour we had made that afternoon, it was clear that there was not just one mood here – each corner had its own atmosphere. We would have to unpick this place stitch by stitch to know how to put it together again.

PRINCIPLES

Creating a garden at Home Farm has not been straightforward and it has taken many hours of soul searching and discussion, and countless days of hard graft, to achieve what is here today. But the process has been the best part of it. We have never been bothered by the fact that the garden has taken over a decade to create and that it is still developing. It has been a slow evolution because it has been gardened in real time, as and when money and labour have been available. We have needed time to find the materials that feel appropriate to the place, as well as time to cultivate and improve the soil, and to choose the plants that feel right in the place. We have needed the comfort of time to ruminate on our choices and to gain confidence in our decisions.

Although the garden is the key to the mood at Home Farm, we have had to be brutal at times to make the shift from wilderness to wildness. We have had to tread a fine line so as not to overwhelm nature and in order to maintain the balance between the areas we are manipulating as garden and those that are maintained as natural habitat. The garden itself is an impression of nature; it uses a different palette of plants but attempts to make them appear as if they had arrived and colonized the place. This contrivance recreates the gentle leafiness on the bank at the back of the house and the open sun-bleached expanse of grasses at the front and it ensures that the boundaries between the wild and the tamed are always blurred.

A paradox is already in place because to create a naturalistic garden, the close weave of vegetation that had taken over had to be disturbed and dominated to a degree. The unkempt scene that we encountered on that first day was an inspiration, but the land had to be scarred for it to be healed again. There would be no point in trying to garden amongst the existing thickets of bramble or with the threat of bindweed and creeping thistle ever present. Control has had to be gained before the blue touch paper of the new garden could be lit. This is the process of garden making.

Order is a very particular thing and one person's idea of control can be very different from someone else's. But control is essential even in a garden that is aping the soft informality of nature. Nature is, after all, brutal and competitive. To clear enough room in which to garden, we had to play the same game. Although the look at Home Farm is undeniably gentle, it belies the strategic planning that was put in place to ensure that *our* chosen balance was maintained. The inner gardens close to the buildings and even the meadows are ordered with a relaxed but rigorous hand, striking at the right point and in the right place. The bindweed and creeping thistle are not welcome here but in the outlying hedgerows and woodland the weeds, which after all are only plants in the wrong place, are given their opportunity to contribute.

Summer cut-back in the Woodland Garden.

Planting Tom's Wood, 1987.

Removing manure from the area that was to become the Barn Garden.

The site of the Woodland Garden, before the digger came in to cut the bank away from the rear of the house.

The digger resculpting the bank to the old orchard.

Building the steps in the Woodland Garden.

The Woodland Garden was dug over and mulched and the paths introduced in the autumn of 1987, whilst renovation work was being carried out on the house.

Steve and Sarah.

To garden with nature, a pact has to be made and this pact is based on common sense. Wherever possible nature is given free rein so that the ecosystem is allowed to develop. We do not use chemicals here and garden on organic principles so that the natural predators are encouraged. The wildlife has increased as the gardens have evolved. There are more birds than before, as well as an increase in the insects that feed them, and there has been a quantum leap in diversity with the advent of the pond.

Plants are chosen that associate happily and on the strict principle that the right plant is put in the right place. Sun-loving plants are planted in full sun and, if the position is dry, drought-tolerant plants will be grown there. The same principles are applied to shade, as well as to areas that are exposed or sheltered. In this way, plants are kept in good condition, which in turn makes them stronger and more able to cope with the elements and the onslaught of pests and diseases.

With nearly two acres of ornamental garden and two wild acres to cultivate on an average of two day's labour a week, we have to be well organized. The secret is to keep an eye on the whole picture and use the labour at the right point and in the right place. We are consummate mulchers. Weeds are never allowed to seed and plants are chosen for their ease of maintenance and planted to cover as much ground as possible to smother any invaders.

As the garden has grown, we have had to increase the time that we spend on it to keep it in good condition and moving forward. Since its conception I have been coming up from London for two to three days a month, but with help with the mulching and pruning from gardening friends at strategic points in the year. When we developed the Barn Garden, I started to bring a gardening friend, Sarah, to help. Four years ago, Steve, a local fireman, came to garden one day a week. He has been a passionate gardener since he was a child and now we could not do without him. The grass is cut by another enthusiast, Bernard from the village. The garden's success is based on both good planning and committed teamwork.

The yew bower in spring.

LOCATION

Although the land attached to Home Farm is no more than four acres, there is such a sense of space that you feel you are in the middle of nowhere. The buildings are cut into a south-facing rise that forms a horseshoe shape in the gently rolling farmland around the rear of the property. The land opens out and down at the front into the head of a shallow valley that moves off and away into ridge-and-furrow fields. It is from this direction that the worst of the winter weather comes, bouncing across the open expanse that runs on into the lowlands to the east.

The property was carefully planned all those years ago. It was built in the eighteenth century and faces due south so it bakes in the summer, while the barn cuts off the east wind. It has the additional protection of a small copse of beech in the north-east corner, affording shelter from the winter winds, while a mixed copse to the west of the house shelters it from the prevailing south-westerlies. Northamptonshire can be a cold and bleak county in the depths of the winter but, even at its most inhospitable, there is always a corner of stillness at Home Farm.

Frosts have been fewer over the past ten years and the winters wet and mild but when cold weather comes, we have experienced temperatures as low as –10°C (14°F) so planting has to accommodate that eventuality. Frost settles in the low-lying ground at the front but tends to roll off the sloping ground of the woodland and vegetable gardens. The ring of trees enclosing this area is also added protection from bad weather.

The soil is a deep, rich, clay loam that is just on the acid side of neutral. Left untended, it bakes and fissures in summer and lies wet but never waterlogged in the winter. We attribute its free-draining nature to the gentle slope and a possible gravel bed that runs along the valley at the front. There is no natural water source on the property, but there are seams of silt in the clay in the lower land at the front that are a possible indication of a past watercourse.

The beech copse (opposite).
The paddock in front of the house before the introduction of the pond (below).

old copse

drive

old ash

tom's wood

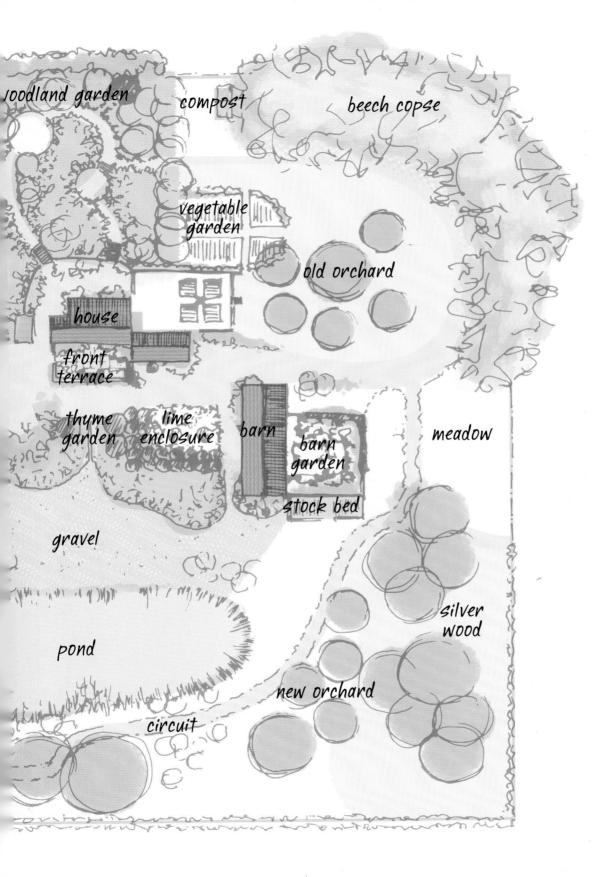

woodland garden

compost

beech copse

vegetable
garden

old orchard

house

front
terrace

thyme
garden

lime
enclosure

barn

barn
garden

meadow

stock bed

gravel

silver
wood

pond

new orchard

circuit

THE NARRATIVE

THE DRIVE

The road peters out to dirt and cracked tarmacadam track once you leave the village and Home Farm lies at the end of that track. Once you pass through the farm gate, a mixed copse to the left of the drive runs along its length and conceals the house from immediate view. The copse belongs to a neighbouring estate, so it is a borrowed pleasure but it is a beautiful place that roars when the wind is high and shelters the house from the prevailing westerlies.

When we arrived, the drive was open, the field that lay to the right panning away to the horizon with nothing more than a solitary ash of considerable age to act as a focal point. Since then, things have changed, both the buildings and the land around them. The drive has been planted to add a feeling of intimacy, a new dry stone wall encloses a terrace at the front of the house, the ash is now reflected in a large sweep of water, and – most importantly – planting unites the buildings.

To change the approach so that the surprise of what lies beyond is revealed only as you reach the head of the drive, the right-hand side of the track was planted with an informal row of balsam poplars. Only nine years old, these are now almost as tall as the old ash and they have a glorious moment in spring when their leaves unfurl and fill the air with a spicy perfume. They have been thinned, so that the row is staggered, and underplanted with an informal hedge of hazel and blossoming trees and shrubs; blackthorn, hawthorn, amelanchier, sweetbriar and some holly for the winter. The ground was sown with a woodland wildflower mix and naturalized with snowdrops and bluebells. Everything is allowed to grow long and soft so that you emerge from the tunnel of poplars and out into the light.

THE TERRACE

When we first arrived, there was a small red brick wall with Victorian railings that bordered a path in front of the house. A small bank that sloped down to the track made the house feel as if it was teetering and adrift. The scale was all wrong and the wall and railings appeared to be tacked on. We quickly realized that the building needed to be anchored to the slope

The pear trees on the bank in the old orchard produce fruit as hard as stones but they are worth the space they occupy for their cloud of spring blossom. They have been interplanted with young greengages and plums.

with an enclosure that was larger and more in keeping with the period of the building.

The old wall and railings were removed and the level extended to a new dry-stone wall that took the summer of 1989 to build. Old gates that had been salvaged from a pile of rust and scraps were reconditioned and hung at two points for access; reclaimed paving slabs were laid to form the terrace and an observation platform within. This place looks out and over the gentle sweep of land in front of the house. The beds around the new enclosure are simply planted so that, seen from outside looking in, the front of the house appears quiet and modest. The base of the wall was sown with wild tree lupins and ox-eye daisies which, over time, have self-sown into the gravel of the drive.

THE WOODLAND GARDEN

The land at the back of the house rises up and away from the Victorian extension to an old laurel and elder hedge. The mixed wood to the west is a significant presence here, contributing to the mood of this part of the garden, so we planted it in a way that feels lush and slightly overgrown. The wood is full of life and, as the sun sweeps round in the afternoon, it casts a dappled shade over much of this garden. An old line of elders encloses this space to the east so that it is almost entirely sheltered from the winds.

The steep bank had to be dug away from the house in the first round of works to make it less overwhelming when seen from the rooms at the back. A curving brick retaining wall separates off a lower area that continues a ring of gravel around the back of the house. Two sets of steps lead up into the garden above and a brick path connects them to make a small circuit that passes through the dense planting rather like an animal track in a glade.

The drive.

The dry-stone wall at the front of the house.

There are two main points of contemplation in this area that allow you to look out over the planting and through chinks in it to the fields beyond. The first is a small circular lawn that is soft and informal. It is a little clearing in the 'undergrowth'. The second is the yew enclosure that forms a contemplative vantage point in the top corner. This area of the garden was planted over three years, starting on the wooded side in the autumn of 1987 and moving out across the garden over the following years.

You can choose to take a small track out of this garden through the five-bar red gate and overhanging elders on to the site of an old pear orchard or you can descend down through the garden to the back of the house and into the lower part of the vegetable garden, which is as close to the kitchen as it could possibly be.

THE VEGETABLE GARDEN

The lower level of the Vegetable Garden was excavated in the second round of works in 1995, the bank being cut away to form a small enclosure that spilled out from the kitchen. This area, full of light and sunshine, is a sheltered place in which we grow the salad crops. There are four main beds connected with a woven hazel arch, while steps lead up to the old pear orchard where the Vegetable Garden was extended three years later. This top level is divided into four unequally sized beds that slope gently to the south and wrap around the lower level. They have been enclosed by a young box hedge that, in time, will be clipped into a soft, rolling form to shelter the young seedlings from spring winds.

The Vegetable Garden has now become a garden very much in its own right: a productive hub that you can look out on to from the kitchen.

The Woodland Garden.

The Vegetable Garden.

THE BARN GARDEN

What was once the milking yard at Home Farm has now become the Barn Garden. Originally walled on three sides and lying to the east of the barn, it had long since fallen into disrepair. The ironstone wall remained intact along one side but had fallen away on the other two into the nettles; hemlock covered the 2.4m (8ft) midden that filled the space inside.

The garden was cleared in 1994, the old wall and heap of manure removed with a digger. Unearthing the old cobbles in the process was as exciting as finding a Roman causeway, their creamy tops like the worn-down teeth of an old animal. The ruined walls gone, we were left with an expanse of land, open to the ridge-and-furrow meadows to the east and sheltered from the west by the rusty bulk of the rear of the barn.

The fallen walls were replaced by a yew hedge that has grown to hide the riot of hot colours that lie within this enclosure. With its feeling of light and air and sunshine, it is a place that could not be more different from the sheltered Woodland Garden at the back of the house.

THE LIME ENCLOSURE

The front of the house has been linked to the barn with an L-shaped planting of limes, intended to feel like the remains of an old building. Planted in 1995, they form a partial enclosure that allows views out between the trunks but retains a sense of enclosure at eye level, particularly when the canopies are in full leaf.

The planting here is soft and informal, with yew forms that offer a link to the trees in the distance and mobile grasses that connect with the fields and the meadowland beyond.

The Barn Garden.

The lower side of the Lime Enclosure.

A breeze often fills this part of the garden with motion. Colour has been deliberately restrained so that the eye can pass freely through the space without too much distraction.

THE THYME LAWN

From the top terrace in front of the house, the view opens out over a low planting of thymes and on to the expanse of water that lies beyond. The swathe of thyme was planted in 1997 with three varieties that flower in sequence over the summer, creating patterns on the ground like the shadows of clouds. For the majority of the year, the low planting retains a muted palette of grey-green that heightens the horizontal lines and embraces the feeling of space here. It is broken by low yew mounds – a reference to the wooded hill beyond – and a narrow path that leads you down to the water.

Below the limes, the thyme planting moves into a low carpet of groundcovers and perennials that sweep around to the front of the barn. A buttress of green and copper beech that will be clipped into plump cushions over time wraps the end of the barn and completes the order of the ornamental planting.

THE WATER

It took twelve years of discussion to build up the confidence to create the expanse of water at the front of the house but it has been the making of the garden. In the winter of 1999, we committed ourselves to realizing our intentions. Although it is still in its infancy, the water has added the heart that the garden needed and already it is attracting a flurry

The Thyme Garden.

The pond in its first season.

of new wildlife. It acts as a mirror to the sky and, as you walk around it, a mirror to the garden as well. Planted entirely with wild plants, it was a deliberate move to integrate wildlife into the garden and the garden into the landscape.

A broad sweep of gravel wraps the ornamental planting in the foreground, replacing the harsh green of the cut grass that previously occupied this space. With ox-eye daisies and corncockle sown broadcast, and randomly planted with dusky stemmed willows, this area will soften in the next few years so that the water is glimpsed through the gauziness of wild flowers and never seen in its entirety.

Behind the water, the willows continue into the meadowland that has been seeded to heal the scar left after the excavation. A small spinney of alders has been planted to integrate the water into the hedgerow and the copse planted in the corner of the property.

THE CIRCUIT AND TOM'S WOOD

The beauty of a walk around the garden is that it is never the same from one day to the next. It is different if it is taken from one direction and then in reverse and it is an experience that can be picked up at any point along the way so that the garden can be unravelled in part or in its entirety.

The circuit expands the experience of the garden and increases the feeling of space; it leaves the ornamental planting behind and allows us the chance to engage with the wilder side of the garden.

A route that starts at the barn meanders through the silver wood and allows a glimpse along the length of the water. A small path cut into the long meadow then passes out to

The beech copse behind the old orchard.

The meadow and silver wood.

The path cut into Tom's Wood.

the far side of the water along a small depression in the land, introduced to make the walk appear a well-trodden path. This path leads on to the jetty, where a view is revealed back across the water to the buildings, and passes from the openness here to the sheltered environs of Tom's Wood.

Tom's Wood was planted the year Tom, Frances's son, was born, in the first year at Home Farm. It lies in the south-east corner of the property and forms an L-shaped section that runs along the boundary. Planted entirely with British native trees, it includes at its far end a small area of about thirty hazel trees that are just starting to be coppiced in rotation, to supply the garden with pea sticks and stakes. It is proof and affirmation that trees are always worth planting; the wait of twelve years feels like nothing now that the former saplings are already towering over our heads. The young trunks are now slender but strong. This place can only get better with time.

When the pond was excavated, a small path was cut into the young copse to allow the circuit to plunge into shade. Cow parsley has taken over from the rank grassland that was here at the beginning, and woodland bulbs and wild flowers are being introduced here to naturalize over time. The walk passes through the coppice at the far end and reunites us at the farm gate at the head of the drive.

British natives are essential to the atmosphere at Home Farm. Meadow grasses, for example, are an inspiration to the ornamental plantings. Young larch were introduced into Tom's Wood as a nurse crop because they are fast growing, but they have been retained for their graceful and significant presence.

JANUARY 1

BALANCE

The garden created over the past twelve years at Home Farm is
the result of a slow evolution. We have had to respond to the land
under our feet and to the environment around us – and that has
taken time. The fact that it has been a slow process, far from being
a problem, has allowed us to grow with the garden. We have needed
that length of time to understand what it means to garden with
the place and not against it.

Rosa x odorata 'Mutabilis'.

JANUARY

A frost on the ridge-and-furrow fields to the east, illuminated by early morning light. The simple post and wire fence contains the sheep that graze the adjoining farm land but allows the garden the freedom of a borrowed landscape.

We have added and taken away, refining both the aesthetic and the way in which the garden is run now and will be run in the future as it changes. But the evolution has worked because it has been underpinned by one simple concept: balance.

Balance has been important on every level. Firstly we have had to strike a balance on a common-sense level, weighing up the odds between what we want to achieve and what is physically possible. The evolution of the garden has been slow, and better for it, because we have learnt to walk the path of least resistance. This has meant working with the soil and climate and the wildlife in the garden.

It has meant that each plant has had to be right for its place and able to cope with the level of attention that we can spare for it. It has meant that when things have not worked, we have had to be ruthless in our response. Some ambitions have proved impossible but when the balance is struck, we have got more, far more, from the garden than we could ever have expected.

The process has involved a great deal of observation: looking to see which way the wind blew, where there was stillness, where the wind would cut quick and cold in the winter and how the sun moved around the trees and the buildings. Despite several years of observation, we still had surprises. Only by being in the Barn Garden in January when a horizontal, ice-laden wind bumps off the fields to the east can you see how very differently this part of the garden needs to be treated from, say, the benign shelter of the Woodland Garden behind the house.

The double white form of the Scotch briar, *Rosa pimpinellifolia*, is in flower for only three weeks but it provides the Woodland Garden with foliage that has a natural feel about it. This is a slow suckering shrub of dense habit forming a mound of 1.5m (5ft) in time.

Beth Chatto's words 'the right plant for the right place', have rung loud and true here and underpin the way in which the garden is run. Shade will be planted with plants that are happy there; sun is planted with sun lovers. Plants that favour dry ground are given just that; those that favour wet are given a moist position rather than watered when they show signs of stress. This is a labour-saving strategy in a labour-intensive garden and we have to be strict to achieve as much as we do in the time available.

We look to nature to give us the clues in the garden, not only in terms of its naturalistic look but also in terms of what will combine with what, and where it will be happiest. In the hedgerows honeysuckle has its feet in the cool and its head in the sunshine so it is given the same treatment in the garden. This considered approach goes for each and every plant. If it does not thrive, it is given another chance elsewhere and the hole it leaves behind replanted with something more appropriate.

The planting palette will immediately start to come together when plants are combined that favour similar conditions. The tough spininess of sea hollies not only *feels* right with the mobile airiness of *Stipa tenuissima*, they are culturally happy together, thriving in sun and growing in poor soil that never sees artificial irrigation. A balance is struck between the plants and their position; they are comfortable in their surroundings and will be all the stronger and better for it.

When planting like with like you must consider the vigour of a plant – a gregarious thug cannot be put alongside something delicate and solitary. Such a short-term partnership would lead either to considerable effort to maintain the balance or the sad demise of the weaker of the two. However, a combination that works in one garden may founder in the next. The eschscholtzias in the Barn Garden thrive among the achilleas in the dry cobbles, but when they get into beds where the soil is better, they will smother everything in their path, and need firm treatment.

Provided you continue to look, the garden will never stop evolving. Sometimes chance happenings create the best companions, which is why it is important to be flexible. The combination in this garden of bergamot and bronze fennel came about as a result of a seedling fennel arriving of its own accord in the bergamot. This combination not only looks right, but the plants are happy in their association too. It takes a certain discipline to keep the balance in a naturalistic garden and the experience to know when to intervene and when to encourage the plants to be themselves, but that is the slow burn of evolution.

When it comes to plant health, tolerance will run short if a plant is not thriving. If this is down to a plant in the wrong position then things can be rectified, but if the plant is being attacked by pests or diseases, positive action is needed. This is the point when decisions will have to be made about the well-being of the whole garden. That includes the flora *and* the fauna. An insecticide designed to kill aphids will also kill their natural predators. The ladybirds and the lacewings will perish along with countless others and that will upset the inherent balance in the garden.

With rare exceptions, the garden at Home Farm is run on organic principles and, as a result, the ecosystem is now very much in evidence. It does demand patience. The predatory hoverflies are now abundant around the marigolds in the vegetable garden, for example, and the aphids consequently in abeyance.

Everything is done to maintain the health and well-being of the whole garden, not just sections of it. But even with plants that are mostly in good health, having the forbearance not to spray has seen us at points under siege from pests and diseases. Mildew and blackspot caused many of the hybrid shrub roses that remained chemical free to be shrouded in grey mildew or defoliated by blackspot. Though their moment of glory was a spectacle for two weeks in high summer, their sad demeanour was a trial for the remaining fifty weeks of the year. Eventually we removed them and the hole that they left has been filled by plants that are naturally healthy, right for their place and happier for it. A balance had been struck.

WINTER SKELETONS

It is all too easy to view winter as a time of hardship, the barren season. The daylight hours are short, the sky a continuous grey that can seem at times to be hovering just out of reach. From the warmth of inside, the garden can appear to have reached stasis.

The garden is, in fact, the very thing that will entice us outside to experience the potency of this season. Braced against the cold and engaging with the garden's new incarnation, it becomes clear that this is just another period of flux. It is a slumber, not a deep sleep.

Gardening on the side of nature, as we do at Home Farm, we leave last year's growth to wind down in its own time. Foliage is left where it falls on the ground, initially for pattern and colour, and then for the goodness that it will return to the soil as worms pull it into their burrows and the bacteria set to work on returning it to the cycle. Leaves are only swept away

Winter stems of *Rosa glauca* and spent seed heads of echinacea.

The chalk-white stems of *Rubus thibetanus*.

from drought-loving plants such as santolina and thyme to prevent them from rotting, or where the wind has drifted them into smothering piles. Clearing leaves from the paths and terraces goes a long way to making the garden feel cared for, the juxtaposition against the spent stems of last season making the contrast keener.

The absence of summer clothing reveals the bones of the garden, in a new and reduced aesthetic. What we are left with at the beginning of the new year, or at the end of the old one, is a newly revealed garden with space and air. Winter forms often bear no resemblance to the voluminous greenery that they sported in the summer. Some, such as *Dicentra spectabilis*, leave no more than a papery sheath, a ghost that is consumed by the season not long after it is felled by frost. Alchemilla leaves a cartwheel tracery of stems where it has collapsed on to paving, staining it with an image of the summer's growth.

Some perennials bestow on the winter garden a skeletal legacy that is every bit as interesting as their summer incarnation. These forms will continue to provide the garden with shape, texture and colour that is far more interesting than the bare earth left behind when ground is cleared prematurely. Plant skeletons play host to frost and trap low shafts of light that would otherwise be lost. They are also host to a wealth of beneficial insects and the birds are pleased to have the winter seed. Many will last well into the spring. Only then will they be cut away to allow the new growth to come through and make way for mulching.

Sedum telephium 'Matrona' with *Molinia caerulea* subsp. *arundinacea* 'Windspiel' in background.

Cornus alba 'Aurea'.

Much of the planting at Home Farm is dominated by perennials and each planting includes something that will endure into the winter months. In the back garden, the great sweep of *Phlomis russeliana* is almost at its best in winter. The tall whirled seed heads will weather wind and snow for a good six months. They are backed in places by bronze fennel that has to be one of the strongest skeletons of all. Frost will re-contour the plant, each flattened seed head forming a platform of ice crystals On a sunny morning after such a frost, the plant gives off its strong smell of aniseed during the thaw.

In the Barn Garden, the hedges become apparent again once the winter takes hold. The giant oat grass, *Stipa gigantea*, will stand tall until it is felled by snow. It is as bright as parchment against the yew hedges when dry, turning a hot cinnamon when wet. This grass and the *Calamagrostis brachytricha*, which is now collapsed and blond, form a luminous foil in dull light for the dark charcoal pokers of the *Digitalis ferruginea*. The darkness of one would be lost without the lightness of the other.

The parchment of the grasses is repeated at the front where the self-sown *Eryngium giganteum* is having one of its better moments. Its spiky forms are at their most interesting when they are growing through the netted skeletons of limonium. *Verbena bonariensis* has also self-sown in this part of the garden and it is stronger for growing harder in the gravel of the drive. It looks wonderful where it traps the spherical heads of *Allium cristophii* that have detached themselves and long since blown into the open.

The spareness of the winter landscape throws the subtlety of the season into relief. It is as if the eye becomes keener with the loss of colour. The area below the lime enclosure is almost at its best in the winter with the great sweep of *Acaena microphylla* 'Kupferteppich' nearly burning in the right light. In some lights it is as rich as a newly ploughed field, in others, it is cool and plummy. *Sedum telephium* 'Matrona', which grows through it, is dark and rich in winter, the trunks of the limes silver and the mounds of yew inky dark in their density. We leave this planting until the very last minute before clearing it for spring.

The landscape around Home Farm is a great inspiration in the winter. It is then at its bleakest and possibly most wonderful, all earth tones and grey skies. But looking in more detail there is colour everywhere. The blackthorn will be studded with navy-blue sloes and, where the birds have passed them by, the scarlet hips of dog-rose shine out in isolation.

The 'Scharlachglut' rose in the Barn Garden is one of the best for retaining its winter hips. The birds will always prefer the hips of *Rosa moyesii* first. In the back garden we also have hips on the large wind-proof *R. virginiana* which, in a cold snap, will be stripped by tits in a day or so.

Seen from a distance there is an impression of colour on some plants that may be less obvious close up. The stems of *Rosa glauca* are deepest violet overlaid with a paler bloom. The older stems will darken to chestnut, which is why we remove a third of the growth each year to encourage the young stems. The winter growths of *R. pimpinellifolia* are almost apricot and there is a dusky purple tint over the copper hazels that strengthens as the catkins lengthen.

Other plants have more obvious winter colour. The tips of *Cornus alba* 'Aurea' are a strong brown-red, fading to green as the stems age. *Cornus alba* 'Kesselringii' is perhaps one of the better cornus, all the more striking for being liquorice black. Its stems are encouraged with an annual pruning of one-third of the growth. Cut to the ground and given a good feed afterwards, new shoots will replenish the old. The cornus lie on the opposite side of the path from the chalk-white-stemmed *Rubus thibetanus*, which has delicate fern-like leaves. This is a much better-behaved plant than its rampant cousin *R. cockburnianus*. It also has bristles where its cousin has talons.

Given enough room, the willows are perhaps one of the most colourful winter stem plants, particularly if you can plant them so that the sun falls on them at the right angle. Side or front lighting will bring out the best colour. I have seen them lost where they were not planted to take advantage of the low winter sun.

Down by the barn we have a small planting of *Salix irrorata* which are pruned hard every third year to encourage the silver stems that make them so wonderful against the lichen-covered wall. *Salix daphnoides* 'Oxford Violet' and *S. daphnoides* 'Aglaia' have been planted around the pond for the dusky haze that they cast in the blond growth of last season's meadow.

Hemerocallis 'Stafford' seedhead in a state of decay.

SOIL

Soil is the very foundation of a garden and the maintenance of its well-being is one of the most important roles we have to play as gardeners. Soil that is in good condition is easier to work. It retains moisture in drought and drains well in deluge. Improved soil will be richer, more nutritious and a better medium for growth. To run your hands through soil when it is in good shape is one of the great pleasures in the garden. A plant growing in good soil conditions will thrive rather than merely exist.

The soil at Home Farm has not been easy and it has taken several years to get to know it and several more to tame it. In the areas around the buildings, the majority of the topsoil was disturbed long ago, the subsoil having been thrown up from the building works.

I shall never forget the yellow clay that we revealed on the bank behind the house. Deep fissures ripped across it in drought and it lay sticky and unworkable at the first sight of rain. The barn yard was full of stones that had been driven into the clay to assure a firm footing for the cattle. Paradoxically, away from the hub of the garden in the outlying fields where we have wanted to put the land down to meadow, the soil was rich and deep, a clay loam that yields dock and nettles that stand 2m (6ft) high. Such is the way of the garden, but every last barrow load of muck and every turn of the spade has been worth the sheer delight of being able to run our hands through the black, nutritious loam we have today.

The first step in good soil maintenance is to make a clean start. When the garden was begun at the back of the house, it was shoulder high in creeping thistle, bramble, dock and couch – all pernicious weeds and all very much in control. It was a head-on battle to start with and three of us spent a month cutting down the undergrowth and ripping into the soil with picks and mattocks. A layer of rotted cow manure was then spread over the surface and the whole area covered with black plastic and left for a year. The derelict house was being renovated so there was no rush to plant.

The following autumn, the black plastic was peeled back to reveal a soil that had the beginnings of something. The worms had begun to pull the manure down into the heavy clay below and the nettles, thistles, couch and dock had perished in their year of darkness. The only survivors were the bell vine and the bindweed. To give the ground the clean start we needed, we resorted to glyphosate, applying it to the young growth of these indomitable weeds once they had regenerated.

Glyphosate has been used only very sparingly at the beginning of projects and only on the most pernicious of perennial weeds in the garden. If there is time, we prefer to use black plastic or old carpet for a season. Grassland that is free of creeping thistle is mown in the autumn and then turned in to the bottom of a trench covered with a layer of manure, to rot down and improve the soil there. As far as we can, we try to work the garden on organic principles now most of the land has been cleared.

Once free of weeds, the soil preparation begins in earnest with the incorporation of organic matter. I have an almost religious reverence for organic matter (humus) and it is incorporated on an annual basis to replenish the goodness that the plants remove and to keep the soil in good condition. On its inclusion even light impoverished sands will retain moisture and heavy clays will be opened up to drain. Earthworms and the essential bacteria that liberate minerals in the soil will flourish provided there is a good humus content. A soil without them is fulfilling only half its potential.

Organic matter is used in several forms in the garden. Cow and horse manure are never applied to the soil unless they are more than six months old, and our own garden compost is left for a year so that it is well rotted down. (If you apply anything that is not thoroughly decomposed, the nitrogen that is needed for the process will be robbed from the soil in order to break down the 'green' matter, so defeating the purpose of applying it in the first place.) We use leafmould as humus to enrich soil that is being planted with woodland plants and lilies and we buy in recycled green waste from the council for an annual mulch to protect the soil surface in late winter.

A new area in the garden will always be single dug to incorporate organic matter a spit deep (the depth of a spade). This will encourage the roots of young plants to travel deep, where the moisture is. We also single dig a third of the vegetable plot each year for the salad crops, legumes and marrows. The remaining two-thirds are forked over at the end of the year so that the winter can break down the heavy clods before spring. In wet weather we stay off the soil altogether, or work on it from boards to spread the weight, as it can easily be compacted and damaged; once the air is pushed out, the structure is destroyed.

Digging *is* hard work but it can be started in early autumn and continued when there is time over the winter, splitting it up between other jobs. The benefit of starting early is that the soil can be subjected to the weathering process of alternate frost and thaw, which breaks down a heavy soil so that by spring it is more workable. Any area that is dug has a single trench one spit deep removed. The contents of this trench will then be deposited at the far end

After a layer of rotted cow manure had been spread over the area at the back of the house it was covered with black plastic and left for a year.

All the green waste from the kitchen goes on to the compost heap with any compostable material from the garden. This includes weeds – except live roots of bindweed, which are burnt – green cuttings over the summer and all the spent growth from the perennials at the end of the winter. The thatch from the meadows is stacked to one side and added in layers so that it does not congest the air flow in the heap. Moisture and warmth are retained with pieces of old carpet laid on top.

There are two heaps, 2.4m (8ft) square. We do not have the time to turn the heaps, but a year is long enough to compost a season's waste, so while one is being filled, the other is decomposing. An earth base allows free movement of earthworms, which do most of the composting work.

Opening up the composted heap in the winter is always very rewarding. The compost is dug into the vegetable garden to improve the soil there. It is also used in planting holes elsewhere but not as a mulch: temperatures in the heap are never high enough to kill weed seeds, which will germinate rapidly on the surface.

of the plot. Organic matter, be it compost or manure, is then worked into the bottom of the trench, the base of the trench forked to loosen it if the soil is compacted. The next trench is then turned in to the first and the process repeated, working across the plot until the pile taken from the initial trench can be turned in to the last. To give it a head start, new planting in established areas will always have some goodness forked into the bottom of the hole or into the top spit in the case of perennials or annuals.

The incorporation of organic matter will improve the texture and structure of the soil but it will not be enough to feed hungry plants year in and year out. We use organic fertilizers to supplement manuring. Organic fertilizers such as bonemeal and blood, fish

and bone feed the soil, not the plant. They are activated by the soil bacteria when the soil warms in spring and liberated when the plants are active so that growth is paced. Inorganic chemical fertilizers are like junk food: they give the plant a quick fix and encourage soft, fleshy growth that is prone to disease and to die-back in winter.

Bonemeal is worked in to the soil at about a handful per square metre when digging, and blood, fish and bone applied at the same rate in the spring to established plantings, taking care that it does not fall on the young vulnerable leaves, which can easily burn. It is often reapplied to flowering shrubs and recurrent roses in July. They will have used large amounts of energy in an early flowering and an additional supplement will give them the strength to throw out strong healthy growth for the following season.

FEBRUARY

FORM

Midwinter can be cruel at Home Farm when icy winds come off the flat lands to the east. With an uninterrupted passage between Russia and here, the easterlies always bring the hardest weather. The Barn Garden is particularly vulnerable and I have memories of working there on one particular day in winter before we planted the hedge. Light snow on a stiff breeze drove horizontally over the ridge-and-furrow fields and spiralled in around the old wall, forming a perfect twister in the corner of the garden.

Snow from the east.

The curve of the yew hedge was cut in a gentle sweep to refer to the distant hills and to invite them into the Barn Garden enclosure. The plain dark form of the hedge is a dramatic background to the winter grasses.

Snow has been rare over the past decade in this area but there is always a flurry that transforms the garden, the unifying shroud revealing the true sparseness of winter. The hills in the distance turn to shades of chalk and the distant woods violet, the sinuous forms of the hedges tracing out lines from the garden into the landscape, mapping the land out and away into the distance. The garden and the landscape register as one, a room shrouded in dust sheets with the doors and windows wide open.

When the distraction of foliage and flower is removed, form really comes into its own. The yew mounds at the front of the house stand still and weighty and the pollarded limbs of the lime enclosure seem only more energetic in their explosion of stems. But it is not only frost and snow that harness these forms. They will catch low, raking shafts of sunlight, that, without a body to fall upon, would travel through the garden, seen but unsung. When the sun is low, shadows many times their true height are cast across the ground.

Uninterrupted by foliage, the structure of the garden is also revealed by the paths, or the re-emergence of the old stone walls. But as the garden does not rely heavily upon the structure of hard landscaping, we have used plants to form its architecture. The formality of the pollarded limes is used to link the buildings, and yews are used to weight them and to create divisions and enclosure.

Plants with strong structure are used as focal points and guides in the garden to draw you through the space and to link the garden with the landscape beyond. They are used as a contrast to the horizontal and vertical planes, and when clipped or pollarded they pull the informality together. They form the bones of the garden – creating a structure that gives the informal cloak of foliage and flower its freedom in the summer and retains interest in the winter.

The yew has been vital as part of the garden's narrative. It is used as a building block to enclose the Barn Garden and to add form and weight to the gardens at the front of the house. The yew hedge in the Barn Garden has several functions. It replaces the line of the old wall, giving a sense of enclosure in this garden, which, despite its naturalistic feel, has a vibrancy that needs some containment, adding a dark foil to the hot colour within. The surprise you feel upon entering an enclosed space adds to the excitement of the garden. In practical terms, it provides a shield from the easterly wind. Although the hedge has to

react as a barrier, it also needs a softness and sensuality that is in keeping with the gently rolling land beyond. So, six years after planting, it has been cut into a gentle sweep, echoing the backdrop of the hills beyond and inviting them into the garden rather than shutting them out. On the outside of the garden, the hedge will eventually be clipped into a great rolling buttress to provide a contrast with our wild flower meadow there.

The yews at the front of the house have two purposes: to balance the weight of the buildings and to provide an anchor point for the informal drifts of perennials. They are placed randomly throughout the enclosure so that as your eye travels through the space, they provide a reference point rather like distant oaks that leapfrog across the fields to the horizon. As the area was developed, lower mounds, 3m (10ft) across, were planted to break free of the enclosure and out into the Thyme Lawn. These were built up with young bushy yew, three plants to 1m (3ft), and allowed to develop as a community, then clipped to form a whole.

Box has been treated in much the same way, with a double row of five plants to 1m (3ft) to create the undulating hedges in the rear garden. With regular summer clipping to encourage dense branching, they will start to register as strong forms in about three years. The process is on-going, as we want them to spill and flow, becoming fatter and more sensual as they age. They will then act as a sculptural contrast to the plants around them that are lighter and more ephemeral. When clipped in late July, the box hedges become islands of order and calm in the looseness of summer's profusion. In winter, they are an effective contrast to the skeletons of dying perennials, which appear like netted veils against their solid weight.

The plants singled out for their form are not only those used to create formality and order. We go to great lengths to ensure that each plant can be allowed to develop its own personality, as even the chaos of nature has its own sense of order. Perennials are never tied up in tight bundles but allowed to grow unhindered. Where they do need support, it is discreet and hidden and used only to prevent them from overhanging a path, for example. Shrubs are encouraged to show their character. The plethora of hazel stems or the arching limbs of white-stemmed rubus have their own beauty, unlike the tortured limbs of traditionally pruned roses – the reason why we banished them. Where we do have roses, we favour those with a more graceful growth and they are pruned by thinning rather than cutting back, so that they appear not to have been managed at all.

At Home Farm trees are usually bought as whips or feathered maidens rather than those that have had their trunks raised. This way we can let their lower limbs develop so that they have a feel of the wild about them. Those with multi-stems, or other idiosyncrasies that will not be problematic, are encouraged to develop character. There is a grace and beauty in imperfection and a weight and clarity in order. For the garden to resonate, we encourage the contrast between the two.

The vertical trunks of the limes and the weight of the yews are at their most potent in winter. One works as contrast to the other.

The yew hedge in the Barn Garden was planted along the line of a former wall. The footings were removed with a digger and the trench re-filled with soil, leaving a gentle mound on which the yew was planted as it hates to be waterlogged.

The hedge of young containerized plants (bare-root plants are never as successful at establishing) was set out in early autumn, at a spacing of 45cm (18in).

In the first two years it was protected with wind-filtering netting, as this is an exposed site. With a spring feed of blood, fish and bone, plus mulching to retain moisture, it grew a foot a year. The sides were cut as usual in August but the top was only tipped to encourage branching and allow it to increase in height. After six years we cut the curve into it, marking it with tape first to ensure that the shape worked with the hills in the background.

PRUNING

Pruning is one of the essential disciplines in the garden. Without it, plants would rapidly outgrow their allotted space. It is also necessary to maintain the plants' health and vigour. But it needs to be carried out with a sensitive hand so that the garden maintains a softness. Each plant has its own character and habit that need to be understood for it not to appear to be ravaged by this intervention, and it has taken a while to develop a pruning style at Home Farm that almost goes unnoticed.

Sometimes, however, the soft informality needs some definition to rein it in; pruning can then be used to inject a sense of order. So there are two pruning regimes at Home Farm, one discreet, the other obvious.

The yew, box and limes fall into the latter category. They create the solid contours in the garden that provide a sense of order – the smooth boulders against which the ebb and flow of informality will wash. The fans of 'Madame Alfred Carrière' roses on the front of the house are also used to bring a sense of tradition to that part of the garden and to indicate that, among the softness and disorder, the garden is still being gardened.

'Madame Alfred Carrière' is unusual at Home Farm because it is one of a limited number of climbers present in the garden. Climbers represent one of the most labour-intensive parts to the garden so they are kept to a minimum but cosseted when they are used. In truth, pruning is time-consuming. In a garden that is governed by the need to cover as much ground as we can in a relatively small amount of time, effort has to be targeted carefully – and that's one of the main reasons why many of the more labour-intensive roses planted when we first arrived were later removed.

Having said that, pruning is a savoured moment, reserved for the times when the ground is either frozen or too wet to work. There is nothing more satisfying than unpicking the tangle of stems to reveal the gleaming, healthy growth in readiness for the season ahead.

Pruning will start in mid-winter when the plants are fully dormant, although with most hardy deciduous plants you can start as soon as the leaves drop in the autumn. The hardiest things are pruned first (along with the vines, which will bleed after February), so that subsequent frost-damage is kept to a minimum. Evergreens are always left until spring as they need their leaves over winter, but pruning is always completed before the sap rises so that vital energies are retained in the plant. Precocious summer-flowering clematis are particularly prone to early growth so they are pruned back hard before the buds swell. In a warm winter this may be as early as the end of January.

Two types of clematis are grown at Home Farm – spring and summer flowering. The alpinas and macropetalas that flower in early spring on last season's growth are only ever pruned to keep them within bounds and this is done as soon as they have flowered, cutting back to healthy new growth. They then have the year ahead to produce flowering growth that will overwinter until the following spring. Then there are those that flower on the same year's wood, such as the viticella varieties and some large-flowered hybrids that are

The young limes (above left) were planted as standards and grown on for two years before they were cut. The limbs were then drastically reduced back to the trunk, to encourage a tight-knit top growth that has a sense of architecture to it.

The limes are pruned every year, just before the buds begin to swell, so that the red stems of the previous year's growth can be enjoyed in the grey months. Hard pruning like this encourages the strong colouring of young stems of *Tilia platyphyllos* 'Rubra'.

Sarah and I take only an afternoon to cut back last year's whippy growth to two buds. Eventually this treatment will result in a sculptural knuckling that will also be interesting in the winter.

Rosa 'Madame Alfred Carrière' (above right) is trained into fans against the wall at the front of the house. The eldest limbs are replaced every few years with younger wood, which flowers better. The previous year's wood is pruned to the fourth or fifth outward-facing bud.

The shrub roses (opposite) are pruned in February, removing a third of the oldest growth to a strong new leader. Sharp tools are essential for this work and in the case of the thorniest roses, these long-handled pruners keep the thorns at arm's length.

used to enliven summer-flowering shrubs that have done their flowering earlier. These clematis are cut back hard to a strong bud at knee height or thereabouts in late winter.

The clematis 'Bill Mackenzie' on the north wall of the house is a tough old thing that is fanned out to the eaves to cover the drain pipes there. I do not want to lose the height and it is now so enormous that it is sheared back like a giant fleece. It does indeed look as naked as a newly shorn sheep, but only for a short while before growth resumes in spring.

Pruning should bring out an exacting streak and a certain ruthlessness. Being decisive is one of the most important things to remember. To do the job well, you first have to

have a feel for the way the plant grows so that you are working with it to harness that energy and direction. This means standing back and assessing the nature of the plant and visualizing the way you want it to look when you are finished. You also need the right tools, well sharpened, so that you are never straining to make a cut. Damaged wood is like an open wound and will attract problems. If secateurs cannot cope, then we use loppers or a small pruning saw. Stout gloves are also important so that you can go into the job with confidence.

Beyond that there are certain pruning rules that are gospel. Always start with the removal of diseased and damaged wood, cutting back to a new or healthy branch. Branches that are crossing or rubbing should be dealt with to maintain both health and aesthetic balance.

Assuming a plant is in good health and that it has the resources it needs, feeding with a slow-release organic fertilizer, such as blood, fish and bone, and mulching after pruning are as important as the activity itself. The harder you prune, the stronger a plant will regrow. The limes are a good example: the trunks stamp a formality on to the ground and their heads are pruned back to tight knuckles to promote the mop shape, which introduces an element of repetition in the informality of the Grass Garden.

The buddleias are also pruned hard to promote strong growth. There are two varieties in the garden, 'White Cloud' and 'Black Knight'. The latter are prone to wind rock, their top growth being wheeled about by winter winds, so they are reduced by a third at the beginning of the winter and then reduced to two buds on the previous seasons growth in February. Hard pruning here promotes long arching growths and good strong flowering. Rules are constantly broken so that the naturalistic feel of the garden can be maintained. For instance, *Cornus alba* 'Kesselringii', which is grown for its liquorice black stems, is never coppiced to the ground in entirety but selectively pruned, a third of the growth being removed each year. The oldest wood is cut away to the very base of the plant with a sharp pruning saw and from that a new generation of stems will push through, blacker and more dramatic for it. We never prune *Rubus thibetanus* at the end of the winter, when we should, but choose to let it flower in early summer, removing all last year's growth as the new is pushing through. It leaves a hole for a few weeks but that is soon filled by the regenerating *Geranium phaeum* that is also recovering from its early summer cutback to promote new foliage.

All the shrub and species roses are pruned in the same manner to keep them in good fettle. Old stems are removed to either a strong new growth or to the base, depending upon the variety. Young growth flowers better, and is also less prone to disease. *Rosa* x *odorata* 'Mutabilis' is the rogue example. It hates to be pruned as there is no rhythm to the twiggy growth, so it is reduced very carefully in height by about a third every other year, maintaining a respect for its idiosyncratic character.

Prunings of *Tilia platyphyllos* 'Rubra'

Snowdrops in the wood are at their best en masse and can be increased easily every year by dividing them in-the-green just as soon as the flowers fade.

PREPARATION

The weather has now begun to take its toll on many of the winter skeletons, some of which have been strewn and flattened by the elements, but among them there are already signs of the first bulbs. The first new generation to emerge are the snowdrops. They are naturalized now on the bank in the Woodland Garden, and this is always the first area to be cleared of debris so that it can be mulched and the bulbs can then grow through the mulch. If you leave the job till they are up, mulching can be very tedious so the green tips of the bulbs are the signal for the spring clear-up – a process that will see the garden transformed.

We start clearing spent perennials first, pruning the woody plants only when the ground is either wet or frozen. The weariest skeletons are removed first and the strongest left until the last minute so that we can savour them for as long as possible. The astrantia stems are one of the first to be cleared, the wheels of last year's leaves have already been consumed into the soil with only the flowering spikes remaining. If you catch them at just the right moment, these old growths come away with either a sharp tug or the combing of a rake but, if there is resistance, it is always best to cut them with secateurs to avoid damaging the dormant crown just below ground.

Good strong skeletons like the bronze fennel and the *Phlomis russeliana* are left until last when last year's dead growth is cut as low as possible to the ground to avoid leaving jagged stumps that will cut and tear your hands later on in the year when weeding. The new growth will soon start to cover the initial nakedness. The grasses, one of the highlights of the winter garden, are also left until the end of the clearing period. Many will stand upright throughout the winter and on into the spring if you let them, but there comes a point when the new growth starts to push through at the base and then the old stems and foliage will have to be cut back or any new shoots will be damaged by your intervention.

The grasses all have their own habits. The deciduous molinias are not the best for winter interest as they are felled by wind early on in the winter but they have charm if there is room, mapping out the direction of the prevailing wind where they fall. They are one of the easiest of the grasses to clear as the growth comes away neatly at the base. *Calamagrostis brachytricha*, however, has to be pulled by hand with sharp tugs to loosen the old growth and *Stipa tenuissima* literally combed out with a rake to clear last year's tangles. The evergreen grasses such as the stipa above and its greater relative, *S. gigantea*, are never

The young tips of *Paeonia* 'Scarlett O' Hara' are vulnerable in early spring and care has to be taken when last year's spent growth is cut away. Much of it will come away easily by hand if it is left until the end of winter, but it will need to be cut close to the ground if it still resists, so that the crowns of the plant are not damaged in any way.

cut to the base. They need their foliage to continue to keep them alive until they start to grow again in April. If you were to cut them, that would be the time to do it but it is really not necessary. We used to cut out each individual flower spike from the *Stipa gigantea* until the plants grew so large that the task became unrealistic. Instead, a shearing just above the foliage leaves them looking shorn for a while, but only until the new flower stems push through.

When clearing on wet soil, we always work from boards to avoid compaction. The debris is raked off and piled high in the compost heap, where it will rot down over the coming year to be re-used in the vegetable garden. Clearing away the spent growth will reveal the young shoots of the seasons to come – scarlet tips of peonies and mossy curled leaves on

Cutting back the old growth on *Sedum telephium* 'Matrona' is left until late. The skeletons are some of the best of all and provide an interesting winter element in this part of the garden.

The grasses are the last of the perennials to be cut back in late winter. Their spent stems add welcome colour and form right through the down season.

the pink cow parsley. It will also expose those opportunistic weeds that have been growing away quite happily during the summer, unnoticed and ready for the off in the spring. Nettles and buttercup are always there to greet you at this moment and should be carefully forked out to remove all the roots. A clean start is essential prior to mulching in the early spring; it also gives us a chance to look at the garden in its true nakedness, the barest it will be for a whole year.

MARCH

3

THE TURNING TIDE

There is a point towards the end of winter when you wake up to different sounds outside. There is a buoyancy in the air that accompanies the lengthening days and gentle warmth in the sun. The hawthorns in the hedges spring to life in places, infusing green into the landscape and the hazel catkins demand that you stand under a nut tree and look up through the pale streamers.

Young shoots of *Paeonia* 'Scarlett O 'Hara' and *Crocosmia* 'Lucifer' in the Barn Garden.

In reality, spring is often still a long haul away, but there is the stirring of life, which can be gathered in an early posy of catkins, primroses, violets and winter honeysuckle. The tide of winter is on the ebb.

The snowdrops on the sunny bank at the back of the house are the first to make a move, and they have been in flower now for almost a month. At their best *en masse*, they are most welcome near the house where they can be seen easily from the windows. Originally there was just a small clump in the hedge line that was rigorously divided in-the-green, just after the flowers faded. Each year at the end of their flowering season, we spend an afternoon increasing the clumps and moving them around the garden. The clumps are split into little clusters of about half a dozen bulbs and drifted informally into their new position, some groups touching the next, others in isolation. This is the best way to increase them as they have time to establish before they die away and you can place them exactly where they are needed.

We have only the wild snowdrop (*Galanthus nivalis*) in large groups. A few of the double-flowered form are planted by the front door where they look most appropriate. The wild form is added to various plantings each year so that they can be enjoyed in combination. They are wonderfully versatile and are just as good in sun as they are in shade. At the front they are planted through an old florists' form of the sweet violet (*Viola odorata*) that was selected for Queen Victoria's glasshouses and originally came as a division from my time at Kew gardens. It is planted at the front by the gate in a hot spot, where in the summer it

Increasing snowdrops in-the-green, just after the flowers have faded, is a more successful method than planting dry bulbs in the autumn. Split into small clumps of six or so bulbs and replanted, they have time to re-establish in their new position before becoming dormant.

is shaded by the *Clerodendron bungei* that grows up through it. It is wonderful in winter sunshine, which heats up the flowers and activates their strong perfume. Passing them on a still day is like walking into a scented room.

In the dry shade under the buddleias, the snowdrops are planted with *Arum italicum* 'Marmoratum', which is at its best in the depths of the winter. This is the marbled form of our native lords and ladies. Its green arum flowers emerge as the leaves are failing in the spring and its toxic berries form an orange club in the autumn, but now it is at its best and it has looked wonderful in this otherwise dead space since early winter. It, too, is divided on an annual basis when in leaf, one clump per year, as it takes a while to settle down.

The dry banks on the exit from the Woodland Garden are lined with large weed-smothering mats of *Symphytum ibericum* and *Vinca minor*. *Narcissus* 'Jenny' is underplanted through the *Rosa glauca* on the right-hand side of the path.

Syringa vulgaris 'Mrs Edward Harding'.

Helleborus guttatus.

Corylus avellana 'Purpurea'.

Helleborus orientalis, a dark form.

Salix irrorata catkins.

Corylus avellana 'Purpurea' catkins.

Sorbus aria 'Lutescens'.

Rheum palmatum 'Atropurpureum'.

Eremurus stenophyllus.

It is used anywhere that looks bare and uninviting, mostly in the gaps that open up under the deciduous shrubs in winter.

As each year passes and experience grows, the amount of bare soil left in winter after the great clear up of last year's spent stems becomes less and less. Much of the Woodland Garden is covered with an eiderdown of perennials that retain their winter foliage. *Tellima grandiflora*, for instance, forms a russet blanket under the copper hazels, which are hung with pink catkins in February. At this moment the subdued undercurrent of colour is perfect under the catkins but later on in the spring, when the tellima is knee-high with lime green bells and the dark leaves of the hazel are just emerging, the combination is electric. 'Purpurea' the copper form of *Corylus avellana* is infinitely preferable to *Corylus maxima* 'Atropurpurea'. It is more open, more graceful, its catkins are more profuse and its leaves are less obviously coloured. We have both in the back garden.

Tiarella cordifolia, another excellent evergreen groundcover, is used to mark the horizontal planes, drifting through the variegated wood sedge (*Luzula sylvatica* 'Marginata') and the golden mounds of *Milium effusum* 'Aureum', which are already stirring a new fresh crop of luminous leaves. Although all three of these will come into their own later in spring, they are planted to flow through and around the hellebores on the bank. Hellebores are good in this elevated position as you can see up into their hooded flowers. Originally planted in the light shade there about ten years ago, they have now made great clumps.

Hellebores are wonderful plants for late winter, lifting the garden out of the gloom. *Helleborus foetidus*, the stinking hellebore, earlier-flowering than H. *orientalis*, the Lenten rose, is in flower in January, its green bells unfurling into a great cluster above the ruff of inky-green leaves. This is one of the best hellebores but it is only short-lived so each year a handful of young self-sown seedlings are dug up and used to replace three year olds that begin to look shabby. They will grow rapidly in the summer to form great shiny mounds of leaves.

The Lenten roses are a race that can spawn obsession. There are whites with a lime reverse, dusky rose and slate grey, then there are the *guttatus* hybrids with spotting in the bell. The seedlings of *H. orientalis* are much slower to flower, involving three years' wait for a good flowering plant, but the wait is worth it, for each generation will throw up a new colour variation. By introducing a couple of plants, such as the spotted *H. orientalis* subsp. *guttatus* and some slate-black hybrids, our range is getting more varied with each year that passes. Forms that we want to retain pure are simply isolated in another part of the garden.

In terms of movement, the buds on many of the woody plants in the garden are beginning to swell, indicating that the sap is rising and the planting and pruning season coming to an end. Without doubt the best at this early moment are the mahogany buds of the *Salix irrorata* that rupture to reveal silken catkins that will turn gold as the pollen emerges. Planted at the back of the barn, their combination of silvered stems and catkins is almost like camouflage against the lichen-covered wall. This is a brief moment but one that can be savoured on the turning point into the next season.

MULCHING

In the gardening calendar, a window opens up after the spent stems of last year have been cut back to make way for the new growth to come. It gives us time to lift and divide any perennials that need it and to complete the planting of new woody material. In a good year, the weather will be kind to us and spring will already be in the air. The soil will be moist and starting to warm up and the first seedlings germinating. Before they get a hold, and the perennials start to swell from their resting crowns, the garden is given its eiderdown of mulch that will leave it looking tucked in and turned down, ready and waiting for the great charge of spring.

Mulching provides vital protection for the soil, which is the very foundation of the garden. Because it is a living organism, it needs a stable environment in which to thrive. We have only to look at natural habitats around us to see that unless there has been severe damage, no place will be without its natural cover. The cover might be stabilizing foliage or the deep leaf-litter of a forest floor. Turn a sod in a field or cut away a bramble-filled corner and new growth will quickly spring forth to heal the scar. As the old saying goes, 'nature abhors a vacuum'.

A soil that is protected will be less prone to erosion from wind and rain. Wind blows away the small soil particles and rain can move soil very easily, particularly on slopes. It also has a pummelling effect and washes away essential nutrients, and can cap and seal the surface. A protected soil will be less prone to drying out, more stable and consequently easier to look after, and better for your plants.

The intervention of gardening can be contrary to the needs of the soil's well-being; for example, when leaf-litter is removed because it looks untidy or soil is left exposed to the elements in the name of order. Our soil has become more retentive and at the same time better drained thanks to the mulch that is applied each year. Every effort is made to take the lead from nature to look after the soil. Soil that is not covered by perennial foliage is left untouched until now so that as much as possible of autumn's leaf-litter is returned to the soil, which is then covered with an organic mulch to protect the surface.

Mulching is one task that is never overlooked in a gardening year. It is the key to being able to garden as intensively as we do. It not only keeps the soil moist and stable, but has the added benefit of smothering any unwanted seed by keeping it in darkness, saving many hours of labour. A bed left free of mulch will very quickly become colonized by seedlings, be it weed-seed that has blown in or seed of self-sown perennials. Soil is left naked only in selected parts of the garden, where the annual black opium poppies and eschscholtzia need the bare soil to re-grow each year. These areas are left undisturbed or mulched carefully once the plants are large enough to cope.

It is important that mulch is put down at the right time. The soil should be damp, so the moisture will be retained and also warm, as the eiderdown of mulch will trap cold as effectively as it will warmth. Late winter or early spring is therefore the ideal time. It is also essential that the soil is free of perennial weeds, which will simply push through and grow the better for it.

In terms of depth, a good 5–10 cm (2–4in) layer spread evenly over the soil will be enough to prevent any weed seedlings from germinating. Big brutes like the Scotch thistle will push through, but can easily be hand-pulled as a mulched soil is a friable one. The mulch should be pushed around the stems of plants, up to the new growth and under the skirts of shrubs. Covering the crowns of plants is fine if they are still dormant but should be avoided if they retain their foliage in winter, so some care is needed.

Depending upon where you live, a mulch can take many forms. It can be compost, manure or leaf litter. It may be that it is easiest to obtain chipped bark or spent hops – the key is that it should always be partially decomposed otherwise it will rob the soil of nitrogen and the garden will suffer. A mulch can also take the form of gravel which, although it will not improve the soil, will protect from erosion and desiccation and can be useful where drought-loving plants are being grown. In the Grass Garden at the front, *Eryngium giganteum* and *Verbena bonariensis* actually prefer the gravel to the heavy clay soil there and will seed themselves prolifically.

Over the years, tons of organic matter have been put on to the soil. Initially we used well-rotted manure (and this is still used around the shrub roses to give them strength). We quickly learned, however, that it had to be clean and weed-free (which goes for all mulches), otherwise we encouraged a new infestation of weed seedlings.

As the garden got bigger, it became increasingly hard work to mulch such large expanses of ground because manure is heavy to move, so other lighter mulches have been tried and tested. Spent mushroom compost was used for two or three years and had the advantage of being light and easy to spread but its lime content meant that it had to be alternated with a lime-free mulch to keep the pH of the soil the same. Over the past few years we have been using recycled green waste bought from the council. It

A full 10-ton truck of mulch delivers recycled compost from the local council. This amount covers all the bare soil in the planted areas.

It is imperative that the mulch is clean and free of weed seeds. It is spread in a layer no less than 5cm (2in) to cover all bare earth, pushed up around the new shoots of the emerging perennials. This depth will seal in any weed seeds and protect the soil from desiccation. Over the year it will be pulled into the soil by earthworms and so improve the humus content.

feels appropriate to be supporting a recycling scheme and it has proved to be the best mulch to date, being both clean and easy to move.

The great steaming heap that is tipped in the drive is a high point at this time of the year. Although the load got bigger and bigger each year, the 40-ton lorry that embedded itself in the drive for a day and for a while looked as if it may have become a permanent fixture, taught us to restrict the delivery to one 10-ton load plus a load of well-rotted manure if we can get hold of it. Now that much of the ground is covered by evergreen perennials that seems to do, but we will use every last barrow-load.

SOWING THE FIRST SEED

As the sun gathers a little more strength and the soil warms, the first seedlings stir in readiness for the growing season ahead. The process of mulching should have capped the soil over to prevent the new progeny, but where the ground is left bare, the first wave of weed seedlings are up. This is an exciting moment that indicates that the ground is getting warm enough to sow the first of the hardy plants. The hardy annuals and wild-flower seed that enjoy an early start can now be sown and there is time enough to plan for the vegetables, which will be sown later when there is guaranteed heat to keep them in constant growth.

As there is yet no greenhouse at Home Farm, the garden is stocked almost entirely with plants that do not need artificial heat. We have three cold frames that act as a half-way house for early sowings in pots and for harbouring new plants in the winter. The frames are then devoted to growing basil for the summer, where the added protection yields far better crops than you would get in a poor year. The decision to limit ourselves in this way is a matter of practicality. Growing plants under glass requires regular input which is not available in the garden: plants have to be able to fend for themselves after initial preparation and targeted input. Of course there are exceptions, such as the tomatoes, sweet peas and early beans that are sown inside, but these are produced in small numbers and held on a windowsill until it is warm enough to put them into the frame to harden off.

The majority of the seed-raised plants are sown directly into the ground. There are two methods for doing this: the vegetables are sown in drills and the hardy annuals broadcast to introduce a random, lived-in feel amongst the borders. Many of the hardy annuals like to be able to get their roots down into the soil whilst it is still reliably moist, to form a good foundation for vigorous top growth later on in the spring.

A good root system is everything. Given this head start, the annuals will be able to compete in the battle that ensues as soon as the perennials really start into growth. The eschscholtzias are a good example. In their wild state in California, they have to seize the opportunity when the ground is moist from winter rains so that by the time the dry season comes, they are ready to flower and spread their seed for another year.

The California poppies in the Barn Garden do not have to be re-seeded now that they have a hold; on the contrary, it is a case of keeping them in control. But the black opium poppies are erratic and need to be re-sown in parts of the Grass Garden. They have a habit of moving from place to place, preferring not to recolonize land in a second year, so some seed is saved to scatter around where they are wanted. If left to their own devices, they always choose the wrong place. Both these hardy annuals appreciate bare ground that has recently been disturbed so that competition is kept to a minimum. This goes for all seed – a clean start is worth striving for. On occasion it may seem onerous, but this is a small part of the bargain. All we have to do is create the right environment for growth.

If left fallow over the winter, ground that was prepared at its onset will have been weathered by the winter frosts, so raking it down to a fine tilth should not be too much of a problem. A fine, even tilth has a texture like the top of an apple crumble – the particles large enough to allow free movement of air and water but small enough to be a good home for seedlings to find a purchase. Waiting for the right conditions to prepare the soil prior to sowing is worth it. The soil should not be so wet that it will be easily compacted, nor should it be so dry that it cannot easily be worked to a crumbly tilth. In dry weather, it is often worth setting a sprinkler on to the plot the day before.

Broadcast sowing is a quick process that involves nothing more than running a hoe or a rake over clean, recently forked ground to create a fine tilth and then scattering the seed over the surface. The fine seed of poppies, verbascum and foxgloves are best sown on the surface and lightly raked in. Larger seed, such as corncockle, can be sown into shallow drills or individually pushed into position using your thumb and forefinger. This sounds labour-intensive but often all that is needed is a smattering of annuals to soften a planting scheme. In more open positions or where larger numbers are needed, drills can be drawn in short rows, spacing them a few inches apart, with the seed never buried more than two to three times its own depth. All seed should be marked to remind you what it is when it emerges; in the frenzy of spring, youngsters can easily be mistaken for weeds.

When the meadows were sown at Home Farm, an early sowing yielded the best results – the seed coming up as soon as it was warm enough for growth. Sowing in autumn gives even better results: the summer heat retained in the soil, coupled with reliable moisture over the autumn and winter, encourages the young seedlings, which are ready come the spring for the year ahead of them.

It is imperative that the soil is clean before sowing takes place. Once a meadow is germinating, it is virtually impossible to go into the sward and pull out persistent perennial weed seedlings such as dock and creeping thistle. Even ground that appears to be weed-free can be harbouring a dormant seed bank that, come the spring, will set into growth to colonize the bare earth. For this reason, meadows are often sown in the spring. Using the winter to allow the residual weed seed to germinate helps to alleviate this problem. Come spring the seedlings are either sprayed off with glyphosate or hoed off to generate a stale seedbed prior to sowing. Although we prefer not to use chemicals, this was one of the rare occasions that their careful use proved necessary.

Meadows are a man-made construction and the best ones are often the oldest. They are rich in flower because the fertility of the soil has been lowered over the years with annual hay cropping and grazing. By removing the vegetation that would decompose into the soil to form humus, nutrient levels become depleted. Many good meadows are also on poor land that is only good enough for grazing.

The soil that favours a good wild-flower meadow is therefore poor and low in nutrients. The majority of the soil in the outlying areas of the garden at Home Farm is precisely the opposite. Good conditions promote the growth of grass, which chokes and suppresses wild flowers, so the best results have been in areas that have been spread with subsoil from

The pepper pot heads of black opium poppies are collected as they split open. They are annuals that like to germinate early in the year so this seed will be stored in the cool, dry cellar and then broadcast in late winter to boost the self-sown colonies at the front of the house.

building excavations. We have also reduced the vigour of the grass by introducing yellow rattle (*Rhinanthus major*), a semi-parasitic annual that feeds on the grass roots.

Once the soil was ready to sow, we waited for a still day and broadcast the new ground at roughly a handful a square metre. You can reduce this to half and sow from two different directions and the chances are that there will be a better seed cover. What you have in your hand looks like very little on the ground but this is one of the wonders of raising plants from seed. A light raking-over will settle the seed and reduce the amount eaten by birds, and the moisture of dew and spring rains will encourage the seedlings to take hold. In good conditions a halo of green will cover the bare earth in a matter of days. All that is needed from this point is patience.

APRIL

SCENT

The sense of smell has both power and subtlety. Of all the senses, it is the one that will dig deep into the memory and play on mood. It can mark a time in the day or an event, being heady and heavy one minute and fugitive the next. It can be deeply affecting, partly no doubt because it is invisible, but a walk in woodland would not be the same without the musky smell of leafmould nor is the picking of fruit the same without the tease of sweet, mouth-watering perfume.

Amelanchier lamarckii with young growth of *Astrantia alba* subsp. *involucrata* at its feet.

The arrival of spring at Home Farm is marked with the unfurling of the balsam poplars on the drive. Their long buds will shed sticky scales in a matter of a few days when the sap has risen. The way they look now, back-lit by afternoon sunshine, is like no other moment in the garden, a copper veil glinting and shimmering overhead. Even more spellbinding is the sweet and spicy perfume of their young growth, caught on the cool spring air.

The balsam poplars were planted along the drive to create a tunnel of foliage from which you emerge into light. They have a special association for me from childhood, reminding me of a place in a river valley near home that would be transformed by a glorious scent for three weeks each spring. I did not know then that the scent came from the poplars, but when I discovered the origin of the perfume, the memory had to be recaptured.

At Home Farm we are lucky enough to be able to plant on a large scale, but even the five trees that are on the driveway are enough to change the mood of the garden in the right moment. From the young whips that were planted in 1990, they have grown up and out and the perfume they cast on to the air has become stronger with each year that passes.

The scent of foliage is fresh and invigorating, very welcome after the introspection of winter. In the spirit of the balsam poplars, sweetbriars are used to carry perfume further into the garden. The sweetbriar (*Rosa rubiginosa*) is a native plant that has been used on the periphery of the garden to blur the boundaries between the wild and the tamed. It is a wonderful rose that, on a moist calm morning or evening, will fill the air with the unmistakable scent of sweet apples.

The perfume does not spring from the flowers, which are fleeting dog-roses. It is the leaves of the sweetbriar that yield up the distinctive perfume – not a smell that you can locate easily, but one that carries on the air. It is the whole plant that is perfumed, scenting the air in great clouds around it. If placed carefully in the garden, these roses will generate a smell that creates the most delightful surprise to stumble upon, a sensory punctuation.

The secret when using any plant that has an ambient perfume is to place it on the windward side of a planting or somewhere that is still and contained. All the sweetbriars are planted on the south-west side of the paths or planting so that the prevailing breeze will capture the scent and carry it into the garden rather than away from it. *Rosa primula*, the incense rose, is another rose used for its scented leaves. The plant is lighter and less vigorous and, because it seems to hate competition, it is grown by the entrance to the Woodland Garden where it marks its territory with a spicy odour. The ferny leaves of the incense rose are sticky to the touch and, unlike the sweetbriar, they seem to hold on to their perfume for the duration of the summer. It has something of sherbet about it that makes your mouth water.

Perfume is used to trigger reaction in the garden, so that even when rushing or passing from one place to another, you are left with a sensation. Voluminous plants such as the poplars or the June-flowering *Elaeagnus* 'Quicksilver' will scent the whole of the driveway and are wonderful for sending perfume across open spaces. Elsewhere in seating areas and close to paths and windows, scent may be used with more intimacy.

Scented *Populus balsamifera* is at its most fragrant when the leaves first unroll in spring. The trees were planted as whips in 1990 and have grown on average about 2m (6½ft) a year, providing an immediate sense of enclosure along the drive. Their roots are far reaching so it is important that they are kept well away from drains and buildings.

Whether the scent is on the air, or crushed between finger and thumb, there is no point in the garden that is neglected. By the front gate we have a large shrub of *Viburnum* x *burkwoodii* that is at its best in spring, with its heavy scent of cloves. Buddleia is planted nearby to take over the role in summer. The sweet violets that underplant them are all the better for being in an area that heats up in sunshine, when the perfume is activated and mobilized. You can walk through it rather than be obliged to get down on your hands and knees to experience it.

Heat and moisture combined are the best conduits for scent. There is nothing quite like opening cold frames full of basil or the smell of the garden after a summer shower of

Viburnum x *burkwoodii* (top) is planted close to the south-facing wall and gate at the front. It is a slow-growing semi-evergreen. The incense rose, *Rosa primula* (above), is also planted by a pathway so that its spicy aromatic foliage can be savoured. It dislikes competition and prefers to be grown on its own.

rain. On a warm evening in mid-summer, the garden will be alive with it. *Lonicera periclymenum* 'Graham Thomas' is grown over the whole of the back of the house in the shade, up and around the windows so that the scent can move freely into the house. The back of the house is still, so the scents are trapped and captive.

By contrast the walls at the front are breezy but they face south and heat up during the day. Come the evening, the warm air that they continue to radiate will activate and intensify scents such as the heady perfume of jasmine and *Lilium regale*. The lilies are always grown in large pots, three to five bulbs to each one, so that come high summer they can be placed as scented punctuation marks on the terraces and near open doors. On a still summer's night, these lilies are capable of scenting the whole garden with their exotic perfume – intense and heady for some, but an indulgence for those who love it.

On a hot day, the garden at the front smells more Mediterranean than English, with the aniseed aroma of fennel, spicy lavender and musky santolina; when the thyme garden is being cut after flowering, the air is full of its scent. After the job is finished, whoever has done the cutting walks around for the remainder of the day with their hands smelling of it.

The garden at the front is one of the few places where we have ornamental roses. Despite the fact that they need so much attention, they are limited to a few of the best and these have been chosen for scent as much as for their looks and good health. *Rosa* 'Stanwell Perpetual' is a particular favourite that blooms early and then continues intermittently during the summer. Each has its own perfume. *Rosa* 'Madame Hardy' is fresh and lemony and 'Madame Alfred Carrière' gentle and sweet. *Rosa gallica* var. *officinalis* (the apothecary rose) and 'Tuscany Superb' are confined to the stock beds as we do not spray for mildew, and these are two of the worst affected. But their scent is exquisite and they are cut in bud and brought inside to be appreciated.

THE VEGETABLE GARDEN

The productivity of the Vegetable Garden sets it apart from the rest of the garden and it demands a degree of maintenance that is higher than anywhere else, but despite this the vegetables are a necessary luxury. For the time that the garden is cropping, this small area produces more than enough organic vegetables and herbs for Frances' family. There is nothing better than having produce in plenty so that herbs can be picked by the handful and salads likewise. What is more, as you eat them within minutes of harvesting, they bear no resemblance to supermarket vegetables. They are plumper and crisper, and the taste is unparalleled, *and* there is also the added knowledge that everything has been picked from the garden.

The Vegetable Garden occupies a prime position in sunshine, the soil is deep and heavy but well drained because it is on the bank. Because vegetables are big feeders, extracting goodness from the soil to yield and crop, great efforts are made to look after the soil here: it is enriched every year with the entire contents of the compost heap. *The Vegetable Garden Displayed*, by Joy Larkcom, and books on organic gardening produced by the Henry Doubleday Research Association, have been a constant source of reference and have provided the best information available on vegetable gardening. Experience of course, follows on a close second.

The garden is currently divided up into two main areas. In one, the little courtyard, the four beds are used for unusual salad crops and herbs. These are the vegetables that are used daily during summer and need to be easily accessible. The centres of the beds are planted with sweet peas or sunflowers so that there is a mix of produce and flowers, and the paths are lined with nasturtiums.

In the other area, on the bank, the garden is divided into rough quadrants which are surrounded by a young box hedge, kept low to shield seedlings from wind. The hedge also provides a boundary that separates the Vegetable Garden from the old orchard around it. The four beds here are divided by a 1m (3ft) wide path that allows free movement through the garden and easy access to the beds. The beds are kept small so that they can be worked and cropped mainly from the paths to avoid unnecessary compaction of the soil.

Crop rotation is one of those traditional gardening practices that has, over time, become gospel. But if you are interested in working with your plants and responding to their individual needs, rules can be broken. For instance, the salad vegetables are kept to the lower beds because they are near the kitchen. Elsewhere, however, we do practise rotation in an effort to avoid the build-up of pests and diseases that can get a hold in the soil if the same groups of plants are grown repeatedly on the same ground. Certain groups are also specific as to the nutrients they extract from the soil and therefore it is best to give the soil time to replenish itself by moving the crops on. (See also Soil, page 48.)

In terms of feeding the soil, legumes (podded vegetables and so on) and salads are gross feeders, while onions and carrots prefer to grow in ground that was enriched with manure the previous season, so crop rotation can also affect methods of soil preparation.

Three main groups of vegetables are grown in this area, so we operate a rough three-

The vegetable garden lies on two levels on the south-facing bank by the house. The soil is free draining and the position sunny enough to grow most crops. Salads are planted in the four beds on the lower level and a crop rotation of the remaining vegetables is practised on the upper level. The four sections are separated by a path lined with *Calendula officinalis* (see previous pages). This is planted to attract hoverflies, whose larvae feed on aphids. The young box hedge that is planted around the upper level (above) will be grown to 45cm (18in). It encloses this area, separating it from the old orchard and will shelter young seedlings from wind as soon as it reaches its intended height.

year cycle. The first group, the legumes, also includes sweetcorn, courgettes and tomatoes. This group will need to be planted in soil that has been trenched with compost or manure. The second group, which will follow the first, comprises the brassicas: cabbages, broccoli and turnips. The third group includes the root crops: potatoes, carrots, beetroot and so on. Both groups two and three prefer soil that has been enriched with compost the previous year so, in theory, only one third of the plot needs to be composted each year.

Of course, it is difficult to be rigorous about the rotation because plants like sweetcorn, tomatoes and courgettes demand a hot, sheltered spot. Carrots prefer a lighter soil and garlic needs a baking to ripen the bulbs. Then there are vegetables such as the asparagus that need to have a bed of their own, as they resent disturbance. A plant that is happy in its position will be less likely to succumb to disease, so the vegetable garden is kept as fluid as possible.

Continuity is one of the most important things in this part of the garden to ensure a regular harvest over the season. Vegetables are notorious for producing glut or famine, so pacing is all important. This means that the garden is carefully planned so that one crop can follow on from the next. The gap that the potatoes leave will be replaced with young broccoli that were sown in June. We also sow successionally so that as one crop comes to fruition there will be another generation waiting in the wings; there will rarely be bare ground left fallow and unproductive.

The year effectively starts in October with the planting of garlic and onions. Planted while the soil is still warm, they will be established by winter and growing strongly by spring to make the most of the sunshine. A couple of rows of broad beans are grown on the same principle. They are quite hardy provided they get established before the cold sets in. The seed potatoes are sprouted in a cool light room in February and planted out at Easter. We grow only earlies because new potatoes are the best of all. There is also always a row of Ratte or Pink Fir Apple because they are less easy to come by in the shops.

The potatoes are sprouted inside in a cool, light room in late winter and planted out at Easter. Their early shoots are protected with fleece until the middle or the end of May to prevent frost damage. Continuity is important in the vegetable garden: over the course of the summer, salad crops are resown every two to three weeks. Lettuce thinnings are carefully dug up and replanted to fill in gaps amongst other vegetables such as the young sweetcorn. In this way, no space is wasted, as lettuce are fast growing and can be harvested young. In high summer the onions, which are grown in the sunniest part of the garden, have their tops bent over to encourage the bulbs to ripen. Once the tops have withered, they will be dug up and left to ripen further, spread out in the sun on the hot slabs at the front of the house.

Inside, tomatoes are sown in March on a warm windowsill to be grown on until May, and then hardened off in the cold frame. Outside, we use cloches to start the salad crops off early, drilling the first rows in April. The salad vegetables will be sown in half-rows every two weeks until the middle of August so that there is a continual succession of young plants. The thinnings will be planted out amongst rows of young beetroot and beans to utilize the space and then harvested young, once the main crops have taken over.

We grow a range of salad vegetables that are not available easily from the shops. Chicory and endive are favoured over lettuce, although we do grow the oak-leaved lettuce and 'Little Gem', both of which taste good and are crisp and hearty. There are always a few rows of cut-and-come-again purslane and Japanese greens, which can be sown as a whole row and selectively hand-picked over the summer. The rows become exhausted if overcropped, so it is always good to have a new row or two coming along in the sidelines. Italian greens

– usually a mix of chicory and cos lettuce with some dandelion and rocket – are another worthwhile salad crop.

Wild rocket is favoured over the cultivated type. It is stronger, more peppery and less prone to flea beetle. Flat-leaved parsley is favoured over the curly type and plain basil is kept in the frames where it is more likely to thrive in a dull summer, as it loves the heat.

As soon as the frosts are over, the tender vegetables are sown directly in situ. The courgettes are sown two seeds to a hole and thinned at the two-leaf stage to one plant per hole. The climbing beans are also planted two to a hole at the base of each cane in the tripod. Leaf beet is sown in one row only as it is a prolific cropper that can be harvested over the whole summer if not overpicked. The dwarf French beans, beetroot, carrots and peas are sown in successional rows two weeks apart, to stagger the cropping.

Picking is one of the most important summer-time activities. It always takes longer than you might imagine but if carried out little and often, it yields the best harvest. Left for too long, the courgettes will turn into marrows and the beans will become woody. Young vegetables nearly always taste better and, with a crop like beans, continual picking will encourage the plant to produce more pods.

ORGANIC GARDENING

Organic gardening at Home Farm has quickly become a way of life that involves looking at the garden from a holistic standpoint. Every attempt has been made to garden with the environment and not against it. Aware that each move we make as gardeners is an intervention in the natural cycle, we try to heal any scars we make or any disturbances to the natural balance. This is far less esoteric than it sounds. Organic gardening is based on common sense and sound practice, doing what is best for the garden *and* for the environment. Of course, the garden is no Utopia, and there are disasters that strike on a regular basis, but we do not regard the garden as a battlefield.

The desire to grow food that was free of insecticides, and grown at its own pace rather than forced with chemical fertilizers, was enough to convince us that the chemical cupboard should remain empty. It was not as if the cupboard had ever been full, but until that point we did use the non-residual herbicide glyphosate to treat the persistent bindweed. This has been necessary in moderation to give us a clean start but now that the garden is up and running, good management and observation take the place of the sprayer.

First and foremost, we garden to promote health. Quite simply this means putting the right plant in the right place so that it will thrive, as plants that are thriving are more resistant to attack from both pests and diseases.

Secondly, the fertility of the soil is constantly replenished with 'natural' products in the form of manures and mulches. We recycle all garden waste where possible in the compost bays so that it is returned to the garden. Organic manure is virtually impossible to buy these days as it is returned to the soil on organic farms but from time to time we do get in a trailer-load of horse manure from the local stables.

A healthy soil releases minerals to the plants as and when they are needed. It is the soil that is fed rather than the plant so quick-fix inorganic fertilizers are never used, because they promote only fleshy growth that is prone to disease and they disturb the natural balance in the soil. Fertilizers are kept to a minimum and those that are used are organic. Blood, fish and bone or bonemeal are added to the Vegetable Garden each year, as an aid to new plantings to get them established and as a supplement to recurrent flowering roses but, beyond that, the natural balance is retained with the use of bulky manures.

Thirdly, we never use insecticides because they very quickly get taken into the food chain and disturb the natural predators that would otherwise maintain the balance in the garden. If there is a severe aphid attack, spraying with soapy water clears it, but generally pests are there to feed the predators. If they are removed, the predators will go elsewhere and then a void is created that will be a rich feeding ground for the pests on their inevitable return.

There has been a policy of encouraging natural insect predators in the garden. Rough areas are left in which ladybirds and lacewings can hibernate and as homes to slug-eating ground beetles. The meadows are left long, as cover for insects and birds, and the wood is kept as a quiet sanctuary for nesting. In it we leave piles of old wood and stones as nesting places for solitary bees and amphibians. The pond has also been a great attraction to frogs and toads, which help to control the slug population, and the Vegetable Garden has been planted with rows of marigolds (*Calendula*), to encourage hoverflies, as their larvae can decimate large aphid colonies. Any flowers with open landing pads, such as fennel and echinacea, are also good pollen centres for the hoverfly.

Where a problem becomes too great it is resolved by getting to its root. The mildew and the blackspot on the roses were a good example. The roses were fit and healthy

Bamboo tripods are constructed each spring for the climbing French beans. Six or seven canes are pushed into the soil and then drawn in and tied with wire near the top. This secures the tripod and forms a wind-resistant structure.

for the first three years but, in time, mildew, rust and blackspot began to build up as spores in the soil that would attack early on in the growing season. A no-spray regime saw those plants that were susceptible ruining the overall picture in the garden so the blighted plants were removed and the holes they left replanted with other things that did better there.

After a time the tree lupins were also removed because of the lupin aphid that arrived to colonize them. This blue-green aphid seemed to have no natural predators and the bushes would hang heavy with them. Ultimately the lupins were burned and three years without them saw the aphids move elsewhere. New plants have now been reintroduced into the gravel where they will be allowed to have their head unless the problem resurfaces. The important point that all the above illustrates is that of flexibility.

One of the biggest problems in the garden are the slugs and snails. Slug pellets have not been an option as they rapidly get back into the food chain, affecting the birds and hedgehogs, which are natural insect killers. A wet year will see snail and slug populations proliferate to alarming proportions – one particularly bad year saw all the sunflowers grazed off overnight, three times. We had to resort to growing them in pots so that they could gain stature before they were planted out. Then a campaign of vigilance had to be maintained involving torch-lit forays to pick off the offenders.

Hand-picking, though time-consuming, is always the best method of snail removal. Slugs are less conspicuous during the day and have presented a greater problem. Beer traps and circles of grit around young seedlings and the bases of clematis, worked in confined spaces. We have also used 'Nemaslug', a product that contains the parasitic nematode *Phasmarhabditis hermaphrodita*. Mixed into a solution of water, this is applied when the soil is moist and between 5 and 20°C (41-68°F); the nematodes kill the slugs, but the slugs remain harmless to the birds. This and upturned half-oranges that were put down as resting places for slugs which were then picked off and disposed of, have worked in the Vegetable Garden, where we do not have to cover too much ground. Out in the main garden it has been easier to resort to using plants that are less susceptible or prone to attack; experimentation being the only way to discover susceptible plants.

Lastly, we remember the motto: prevention is better than cure. The cabbage-white butterflies are kept off the brassicas, and the carrot fly off the carrots with a protective covering of fleece. However, both crops have to be moved around the plot from year to year with this technique, as the pupae, if they are present, can live in the soil and will emerge from underneath the fleece. We also use companion cropping, using basil near the carrots to deter the carrot flies with its pungent aroma. A subscription to the Soil Association also keeps things up to date and on a course that is more about cooperation than domination.

Climbing French bean 'Viola Cornetti'.

Calendula (left) are used to encourage predatory hoverfly and snails are handpicked as they are resistant to the phasmarhabditis that is watered on the vegetable garden to control the slugs. The vegetables are always washed in water that has had a teaspoonful of salt thrown into it to clear any foreign bodies – a preferable option to spraying and ending up with bugs in the salad. One of the best aspects of growing your own vegetables is the opportunity to experiment with varieties not available over the counter. Mustard greens (right) add a hot spiciness to salads and can be resown over the summer to provide a continual succession of young leaves. As with most salad crops, it is best to pick individual leaves rather than the whole plant.

MAY

5

SHADE

There is a tangible rush in the air when the buds begin to burst. It is then that the real eruption takes place, a flood of green rearing up from bare earth. You are ankle-deep in vegetation one day, knee-deep the next. The shimmer of green rushes across the hedgerows and draws across the tree canopy above. The bare branches unravel their foliage in a voluminous flurry and the Woodland Garden underneath is plunged into shade, once again, until summer is over.

Goat's beard (*Aruncus dioicus*) in the Woodland Garden.

The Woodland Garden as seen from the bedroom windows at the back of the house. The copper hazels, *Cotinus coggygria* 'Royal Purple' and purple sage add depth in terms of colour; *Sorbus aria* 'Lutescens' in the background adds light. In the centre *Rosa* x *odorata* 'Mutabilis' is beginning to flower, with bronze fennel at its base. A great drift of *Phlomis russeliana* unites the planting from left to right.

The Woodland Garden has been in motion now for the best part of three months, since the first stirrings of the early snowdrops. They were joined very quickly by other opportunists that put on a spurt of early growth in the race to steal the first rays of sunshine. The hellebores took over from the snowdrops and *Pulmonaria* 'Sissinghurst White' has freckled both sides of the path, leapfrogging and self-seeding into crevices amongst the dark evergreen of the wood-sedge (*Luzula sylvatica*). At this point most of the activity was confined to the floor, but the pace has been gathering as the trees overhead muster their strength, with the sap flooding into their limbs.

The garden at the back of the house has been called the Woodland Garden because of the influence of the old wood next door. It must be about a hundred years old and leans into the garden, sheltering us from the west. The fact that this part of the garden is shaded during summer has not been a problem. Gardening in the shade has given us the opportunity to use plants that stir early and in so doing infuse the garden with early life. The challenge has been to maintain the interest throughout the season so that the early start does not leave this part of the garden feeling spent. The secret of the success here has been to emulate the woodland floor, the ground covered with a constant eiderdown of interest that gives way to a succession of plants, which emerge through it over the season.

The area in the wake of the trees was planted first, using the woodland as inspiration. Varieties of native plants, or plants that felt appropriate, helped to merge the garden with the wild of the wood beyond. The copper-leaved hazel, the amber-berried form of guelder rose (*Viburnum opulus* 'Xanthocarpum') and the white-leaved bramble *(Rubus thibetanus)* were planted in groups, encouraging the impression that the wood had begun to creep out into the garden space. In time, as they grew up, they introduced a sense of intrigue along the little pathway and gave a structure that could be interplanted at a lower level.

The Woodland Garden (opposite) with copper-leaved *Corylus avellana* 'Purpurea' in the background, *Viburnum opulus* 'Xanthocarpum' to the left of the path and *Cornus alba* 'Kesselringii' to the right. Ragged robin has seeded into the path and through *Chaerophyllum hirsutum* 'Roseum' and *Persicaria bistorta* 'Superba' grows under the hazel. *Dicentra spectabilis* 'Alba' and low-flowering *Geranium macrorrhizum* 'Album' will soon be overshadowed by the taller goat's beard. The juxtaposition of foliage (above) provides rich contrast between large-leaved *Rheum palmatum*, hart's-tongue fern (*Asplenium scolopendrium*), *Thalictrum aquilegifolium* and pale light-filled *Milium effusum* 'Aureum'. White-flowered ranunculus and *Galium odoratum* add a sparkle in the shade.

They were joined by other plants that appeared to have spilled out from a hedgerow, plants that had a gentle feel about them and that were happy to live in shade. *Rubus* 'Benenden' was planted on the bank so that it would arch out from the elders there. It threw out 3m (10ft) snaking limbs in the first season and gave us the framework for the golden hop (*Humulus lupulus* 'Aureus') to scramble through. The hop, happy to have its feet in shade and its head in more light, has infused this dark corner with a feeling of sunlight. Though it will not colour well if it is grown in complete shade, it is happiest with a little shade from the heat of the

Yellow-leaved *Cornus alba* 'Aurea' (top), with the male fern (*Dryopteris filix-mas*), dark-leafed *Lysimachia ciliata* 'Firecracker', *Epimedium* x *perralchicum* and silver foliage of *Salix lanata*. Golden hop (*Humulus lupulus* 'Aureus'), growing through *Rubus* 'Benenden' (above).

mid–day sun, which can scorch its leaves. Being herbaceous by nature, it is important to pull it away from the rubus in late winter, to give it a clean start at the beginning of the season.

There are also ferns in this garden, which add a grace and a cool mood to the planting. The male fern (*Dryopteris filix-mas*) is used in large clumps to emerge from lower groundcover, such as *Epimedium* x *perralchicum*. This fern is a strong plant that is always reliable in dry shade and lovely to look at, even when crumpled by the winter. Its bronzed fronds can be cut and used as protection in a hard winter for more tender plants, such as melianthus or eremurus shoots. The hart's-tongue fern, another British native, has been found a place on the bank amongst the *Galium odoratum*. This fern has the advantage of being evergreen, so it is an excellent choice for the winter. It needs a little more moisture than the male fern, but will be content with shade. Ferns are a must in a cool planting.

The perennial layer in the planting gave us the chance to connect all the shrubs and to bridge the path. A limited palette of compatible plants was chosen for the lowest layer of interest, the groundcover. Wood-sedge (*Luzula sylvatica* 'Marginata') was used in large groups with satellite groups breaking away and crossing the path as if self-sown. Originally it was interplanted with *Galium odoratum*, but the rich soil brought out the thug in the galium, which had to be given a position elsewhere in drier root-infested soil underneath the rubus to keep it in check. It was replaced instead with *Tiarella cordifolia*, another evergreen groundcover that can move freely without smothering its neighbours. *Pulmonaria* 'Sissinghurst White' was added, as much for its silvered leaves that are speckled with green, as for its white flowers. The leaves give the planting a lift, a sense of dappled shade even when the sun is not out.

The pulmonaria is broken up by the white form of *Dicentra spectabilis* 'Alba', which likes the coolness here, and by the white *Geranium macrorrhizum* 'Album'. This geranium is in fact pale shell-pink in bloom, but it is a wonderful plant, creeping along the ground on perennial stems that from time to time can be broken off and reinserted into the soil elsewhere to increase the clump. Its aromatic, felted leaves are almost evergreen, so the plant will never look redundant in winter. It is an excellent groundcover plant and is very happy in dry shade. We have the magenta form of it, 'Bevan's Variety', growing at the base of *Veronicastrum* 'Fascination' and *Astrantia major* 'Roma' (one of Piet Oudolf's best recurrent forms). The geranium is excellent because it is happy in combination with its more lofty neighbours and yet is totally weed suppressing. Its foliage keeps the ground cool without demanding masses of water, so the moisture-loving partners in this association are contented, too.

Other plants with a sense of drama were then broken into this cover to add the essential cool leafiness: *Helleborus foetidus* for its sculptural winter foliage and flowers, the giant-leaved *Rheum palmatum rubrum*, and *Aruncus dioicus*, the goat's beard. These plants have a very strong presence, and although the hellebore will be happy to live in limited space, the other two both need room, with 1m (3ft) at least between plants. They also prefer the ground to be on the moist side, but we have got round this by growing them in partial shade. The great difference comes in the time they take to establish. The rheum will rear up into a great leafy mound in year one and has immediate impact, so much so that it can often initially dwarf its neighbours. It has been planted with the white-flowering currant *Ribes sanguineum* 'Tydeman's White', so that its early red shoots have the sparkle of white around them. The aruncus takes at least three years to get going, which I found tedious at first, but with mulching and patience they are now 2m (6½ft) and spectacular in June with their cream plumage. They are used to provide volume, yet there is still a lightness about them.

Bowle's golden grass (*Milium effusum* 'Aureum') is also used to infuse light into the planting. This easy grass is light on its feet, seeding around when it is happy and flowering early in the season, a net of incandescence. Like the hop, the grass will turn darker green in shade and be less

The small meadow in June (top). Once the wild flowers in it have seeded, it is cleared so that it becomes a contrast to the proliferation of growth all about it.

Young leaves of *Rodgersia podophylla* (above). Grown in a semi-shaded spot, this moisture lover will be quite happy. The leaves can burn and scorch in sunshine if there is not sufficient moisture at the root.

interesting for it, so dappled sunlight is the best position. When in flower, the netting it forms makes a wonderful host for emergent plants that appear to hover among it. *Thalictrum aquilegifolium* is spotted through this part of the planting, its froth of violet flowers emerging early in summer above blue-green leaves. This is an easy and long-lived plant, as good in seed as it is in flower, and quite happy in the company of the tiarella at its feet.

Pink cow parsley (*Chaerophyllum hirsutum* 'Roseum') emerges from the groundcover further down the path, on both sides, in a cloud inspired by the native cow parsley in the

Tellima grandiflora (below) forms a weed-suppressing groundcover in the dry shade of the copper hazel. This is a reliable evergreen that flowers early with spires of scented green bells.
In late spring the Woodland Garden (previous pages) is at its most opulent. White spires of *Camassia leichtlinii* 'Alba' light up the dark-foliaged lysimachia and *Cornus alba* 'Aurea' lends a hint of sunlight.

hedgerows. It marks the moment when you wish the roller-coaster of early summer would stop so that you can take it all in. As soon as the cow parsley has flowered it is cut to the base along with the *Geranium phaeum* 'Samobor', to encourage new growth.

The beauty of any shade planting lies in its sense of calm and the cool it offers. It is the place to retreat to when the light has flattened the garden in the middle of the day. You do not demand a riot of interest; what you expect is quiet. The contrasting textures and greens of the leaves are almost enough, once the rest of the garden kicks in beyond the shade. As the season progresses, violet and white are used in the planting to inject little jewels of interest. The violet hovers in low light while the white sparkles and keeps the planting looking fresh. White martagon lilies mark high summer and the interest is taken on with *Geranium procurrens*, which scrambles over the surface, speckling the ground well into autumn with violet flowers, each with a focusing magenta eye. *Persicaria amplexicaulis* 'Alba' is a companion to it, scoring pale vertical lines of white into the planting. This plant does not have the vigour of the more common red and pink forms but it is worth the effort. As long as it is not overwhelmed by neighbours, it is more than happy in the calm that has descended.

ROSES

Not long after the garden at the back of the house was cleared, an order for shrub roses was put together. The light soil and confines of the previous London garden had prevented them from being planted there, but with a heavy clay loam, sunshine and the freedom of space at Home Farm, there seemed to be no reason to hold back. The roses could be allowed to fill out and be themselves; they would be informal and magnificent, bringing with them a certain timelessness.

Their selection became something of an obsession and I was very quickly seduced by the mystique that surrounds them. The garden seemed to get smaller and smaller as the list grew. There were the climbers and the ramblers, the gallicas, noisettes, moss roses and damasks to consider. Then there were species roses in their abundance and infinite variety. The palette soon began to look confused.

Twelve years on, the roses at Home Farm represent some of the toughest lessons we learned, in both restraint and also rigour. In truth less than half the roses originally ordered are still in place. Some have been dug up and passed on to friends, others now reside in the stock bed for cutting only. The ones that survive have done so first and foremost because they are appropriate and secondly because they offer up more than two weeks of interest. A wet June need not be the end of the rose season.

The survivors carry with them a feeling of well-being brought about by strong growth and vigour. The difference between a rose that is flourishing and one that is merely getting by, is vast. Although they may be brief in flower, they have foliage that is both disease resistant,

Rosa 'Stanwell Perpetual'
(top) with *Anthriscus
sylvestris* 'Ravenswing'.
The double white form of
Rosa pimpinellifolia (above).
Rosa glauca (opposite).

handsome in itself and possibly scented. Many also have hips to extend the season from summer into winter. Finally they will have enough grace to blend and merge with the prevailing informality of the rest of the planting, which always errs on the wild side.

After the first four years, the garden was beginning to acquire a balance that prompted us to reconsider the initial rose planting. The gallicas repeatedly succumbed to mildew, if not before flowering, then not long after. 'Pax' suffered from blackspot and some of the albas attracted rust. This rapidly became an increasing problem as the spores built up in soil which, until that point, had been rose-free. The decision not to spray further exacerbated the dishevelment that soon began to irritate. In addition, the appearance of those that needed traditional winter pruning began to look out of place – their angular winter forms standing out amongst the softness of the surrounding planting. I also began to resent the two days that it took to get them to this angular and inappropriate condition, when the same time could be spent achieving a lot more elsewhere.

Certain favourites have, of course, survived the cull. 'Nevada', which is prone to blackspot, is kept in good condition, fed well with blood, fish and bonemeal in March and then given a collar of manure to keep it strong, so that it is able to withstand the third that is removed each winter to encourage new growth from the base. After three seasons, the old wands of growth become tangled and weak and prone to disease. They are removed to the base or a strong new growth low down to keep the plant in fine fettle. All the shrub roses are given a similar treatment and those that are recurrent given an additional feed in early July.

The climbing 'Madame Alfred Carrière' is one of the few roses that are pruned in the conventional sense. The day spent in mid-winter pruning the twin plants into fans on either side of the front door is a joy. The end result helps to give just enough of an impression that the garden is 'gardened' up by the house. In June the arching growth spills out from the wall with a profusion of uncomplicated cream flowers, repeated intermittently until December. The strong

Rosa x *odorata* 'Mutabilis'
(top).
Rosa moyesii (above).

growth of the rose is a supporting framework for *Clematis viticella* 'Purpurea Plena Elegans'.

Other climbers are given free rein to ramble over their supports. 'Wedding Day' and 'Bobbie James' were planted a small distance away from the trunks of the old barren pear trees, trained into position and then allowed to scramble at will. One follows on from the next in high summer, pale cream fading to pink. The double blossom of 'Bobbie James' is more flouncy than the single flowers of its partner but the combination works because it is always seen *en masse* and appears as a great cloud in the old orchard. The scent on the air is a joy and the moment when the blossom drops and falls to carpet the ground is just as captivating.

Most of the other roses in the garden are species, or near varieties of them. The local hedgerow roses provided the lead here and were the inspiration behind the large clumps of sweetbriar (*R. rubiginosa*), that are planted on the boundary between the cultivated and the wild to merge the garden into its surroundings. The sweetbriar is delicious from the moment its apple-scented leaves emerge, to the point at which the birds take the hips in the winter.

Rosa glauca, in contrast, is grown closer to the heart of the garden as its smoky foliage is obviously more ornamental and needs the companionship of garden plants such as echinacea and thalictrum to give it a context. Likewise, *Rosa moyesii* needs the juxtaposition and anchor of other fiery plants in the Barn Garden, but its leaves are still small and the growth loose and arching. This has to be one of the best hip-bearing roses. By mid-August the long flagon-like hips are already imbued with apricot, which eventually turns to scarlet – a luminous end to the season.

More ornamental still in its own delicate way is *Rosa* x *odorata* 'Mutabilis'. This strange rose, historically always listed as tender, was a risk here in the Midlands, but it has demonstrated the shelter that the wood gives to the rear garden. It has also been the inspiration for the plants around it and is now the hub of the planting in this area. Despite

Rosa 'Scharlachglut' with *Stipa gigantea* in the Barn Garden. Although this rose flowers only once, it goes on to produce rounded scarlet hips that last well into late winter.

the fact that this rose is deeply ornamental – the individual flowers fade from cream to apricot to a hot cerise before they fall – it has a wild, untamed feel. We fell under its spell from day one and remain converted.

CONTINUITY

By the end of May, the garden has changed beyond all recognition – it has ballooned out and the whole scale has altered. Where just weeks before there was a transparency, with the trees and shrubs unfurnished, the new growth now is weighty by comparison. All the lines are softened, the paths become tracks through foliage; fresh, pristine and full of life. At times the abundance can make you feel very small but the garden is full and shining.

The lilac is in full bloom against the barn and the ox-eye daisies a brilliant white froth in the gravel along the drive. The box forms have grown their new halo of luminous emerald green foliage. They glow as if from within. On the bank at the back of the house, the ruby-red *Cirsium rivulare* 'Atropurpureum' has reared up to shoulder-height through the young growth of *Cotinus coggygria* 'Royal Purple'. Deepest blue bearded iris and dusky white oriental poppies are linked with *Allium hollandicum* 'Purple Sensation', the first and richest of the ornamental onions in bloom. The tall flower heads teeter above and amongst the planting to unify the area. Meanwhile the thistles give this part of the garden a feel of the wild despite the opulence of the planting.

Although the garden can appear to be at its best at the beginning of summer, this is no time to relax. The luxuriance of this moment can easily give way to disappointment later when the riot of high summer is spent. The garden needs to be planned for each week of the year so that one thing can run into and take over from the next. This means that the planting has to be paced, early performers put alongside slow-burners that will be developing for later effect. The alliums come early, for instance, their leaves up and feeding before the perennials have taken the floor space, by which time the bulbs are replenished for the next year. Then, by the time the poppies and the alliums are over, their place is taken by buddleia and persicaria. Even though the look is soft and naturalistic, the planting is always planned to give continuity.

Continuity is one of the great challenges in gardening. It demands rigour. The ornamental garden would be like the harvest in the Vegetable Garden – glut or famine if not planned properly. You can compare the regular sowings of lettuce, for example, which see several generations, with the equivalent event or happening in the ornamental garden. As one species comes to maturity, another will replace it.

To maintain the continuity, we sometimes have to be ruthless, opening up a gap in the planting when it is at its best in order replant for the future. It feels like taking two steps backwards for one forwards, but the growing season is long and the rewards can be plentiful. The space that the oriental poppies leave behind after they have flowered is a good example. By mid-summer they will have collapsed, their foliage having withered away. Invariably, they will also have slumped on to neighbours so the gap that is left behind can leave a toothless space in the planting. Where red poppies are used in the Barn Garden, the hole is avoided with an interplanting of pot-grown *Helianthus* 'Velvet Queen'. The sunflowers are raised in the frames and planted into the gap to cover for the dormant poppies, so that this part of the garden is given a second wave of interest. *Dahlia* 'Bishop of Llandaff' is used in the same way; the tubers started off in pots and planted out once the risk of frost is past in late May.

Papaver orientale 'Perry's White' with *Allium hollandicum* 'Purple Sensation' in the background.

Iris 'Deep Black' with *Rosa glauca* and *Allium hollandicum* 'Purple Sensation'.

Interplanting in mid-season is not a luxury we indulge in elsewhere. Energies have to be conserved so, on the whole, the garden is planted with a mix of permanent perennials and bulbs to save time potting and watering youngsters. But to keep the garden looking fresh this demands that plantings are given different treatment. The herbaceous geraniums that have already bloomed are cut back hard, along with the *Chaerophyllum*, as soon as they have flowered. Left to their own devices, they would sprawl, their spent stems withering in high summer to lower the tone of the garden. These are not plants that have striking or enduring skeletons, so they are razed to the ground and added to the compost heap. Although they leave behind a horrible gap, the new growth will come back to heal the scar within days, if the soil is moist, replenishing the garden with fresh foliage that will endure into the autumn. If the ground is dry, then we will irrigate to promote new growth.

The well-being of the garden becomes increasingly important as wear and tear assert themselves over the season. A healthy garden in which the plants look good and fresh is the ultimate aim. The roses are given their second feed after they have finished their first flush of flowers, a handful of blood, fish and bone to each, scattered over the root-zone. The garden is also watered if it begins to flag but we do go to great lengths to avoid watering, limiting the hose to the Vegetable Garden and the new plantings. If the right plant is chosen for the right place, in theory it should not need artificial watering. However, with the sunflowers for instance or when the ground is dry after cutting back the geraniums, these plants will need the extra help to put on new growth.

When we do water, it is never little and often. This will only bring the roots to the surface, making them still more prone to drying out. The right way to water is to give the ground a thorough soak when plants begin to show signs of stress, so that the soil is wetted deep down. The water will remain there longer, particularly in a soil that is mulched, and the roots will travel down to find it.

Helianthus 'Velvet Queen' is grown from seed each year in pots and planted out in June in the Barn Garden to fill the gap that the oriental poppies leave behind. They will continue to flower from July until the first frosts.

Maintaining a sense of order is all part of maintaining continuity. *Rosa* 'Madame Alfred Carrière' will have its longest limbs tied in as they grow away from their wires and the clematis are always eased on to their supports and tied in early on in the year. Once they get a foot-hold in the wrong direction, they are too brittle to move. Paths will be mown into the meadows, the juxtaposition of the tamed and untamed indicating a degree of care. It is like combing a parting into the meadow – a simple device but one that works. When the garden is at its woolliest, these things will go a long way to make it feel that it has life in it yet.

JUNE

ASSOCIATION

This is perhaps one of the most glorious points in the year. The shrubs of *Elaeagnus* 'Quicksilver' are smothered in tiny lime-green flowers that throw a rich sweet scent on to the air. There is a freshness and vitality to the foliage in the garden, which is young and unblemished; the beds are full and yet there is still potential for more to unfold in the summer ahead.

Paeonia 'Scarlett O Hara' in bud.

Two giant pots are planted with *Brunnera macrophylla*, which also grows in the gravel at their base. Brunnera has a long season: after it flowers, the leaves remain in good condition, and it is an ideal plant for dry shade.

This is the moment when you can stand back and see the fruits of hard labour, all the individual plants pulling alongside each other, working together in association to make the whole.

Each garden at Home Farm is built around a series of moods, each particular to the individual place. The Woodland Garden at the rear of the house has a feeling of calm and a lushness that is specific to it. The Barn Garden is all about light and heat while the gardens at the front capture a feeling of openness – they are about the breeze, the view and the rolling landscape.

The overwhelming feeling is one of informality, a contrivance of nature that sees us selecting plants that are happy together, setting them in place and then letting them develop without much interference. We, the gardeners, are then responsible for gently steering what develops.

The plants used to capture these moods are as important as the way in which they are put together. Although these combinations can often be no more than two or three different plants, each is working hard in association, living happily in its position and with its companion species.

The plantings are hinged around static elements, such as the yew mounds and shrubs, which act as anchors. Around them there are perennial plants that emerge and retreat over the seasons; others migrate in and out of the picture because they have a shorter life cycle.

Some plantings are more stable than others. The elaeagnus and the lavender at the front of the house are a good example. They are contented in each other's company and remain where they are, growing more informally over time but in much the same place. But a fugitive element adds to the interest so that the planting will never be the same from one year to the next.

Bronze fennel and verbena provide an ebb and flow over the year. At this time, the fennel is dark against the silver elaeagnus but later in the summer it will form a saffron cage of flowers that will be spangled with the violet verbena. Magenta *Lychnis coronaria* wields a punch to make

At the front of the house, bronze fennel and *Verbena bonariensis* are allowed to seed into the hot gravel at the base of *Elaeagnus* 'Quicksilver'. This is a planting that positively thrives in a hot dry position in full sun.

the planting sing. The more mobile elements are hauled back in places if the planting starts to get out of balance, a simple task that takes just half an hour or so a year.

The gravel area at the rear of the house works in much the same way, though the look is very much cooler. It is at its best in high summer with a froth of *Alchemilla mollis* that turns acid green in flower. This planting is, in fact, very simple. First and foremost it relies upon plants that are happy on the north side of the house. Secondly, all the plants capture the mood of the place, which is cool, calm and still. It was laid out very simply at the beginning with a large stand of bamboo, *Phyllostachys viridiglaucescens,* to provide weight to the Victorian extension but with a certain lightness because it is in continual motion.

Bamboo is one of the least appropriate plants for the Northamptonshire landscape but this corner is contained by the Victorian extension and the walls holding up the bank.

At the rear of the house, *Alchemilla mollis* forms the groundcover and *Angelica archangelica* is allowed to seed about as an incidental. It can be pulled where it is not needed. *Viburnum tinus* and *Aralia elata* form the dark structure and *Cornus alba* 'Aurea' lights up the bank in the background. Male ferns and *Lupinus arboreus* punctuate the alchemilla.

The period of the extension allowed us to be more ornamental here and justified the use of ferns and evergreens, while the planting further away from the house is naturally influenced more by the countryside.

The bamboo was planted in deep, rich soil in the most sheltered spot, as it loathes the wind. Its evergreen nature was balanced by a grouping of *Viburnum tinus* that was laid out on the lower level and jumped to the bank, to bridge the two areas. An evergreen that would match the mood of the building, the viburnum provides a stillness that counterbalances the restless bamboo. Both these plants gave us an anchor for more transitory plants. A group of four *Aralia elata* were planted, three together, one alone, on the other side of the steps, to grow up and arch. The lush growth is held aloft on knobbly trunks so there is a lightness to the planting. The brilliant green of *Cornus alba* 'Aurea' on the bank above helps to throw the dark greens into relief.

After about five years, the aralias had soared to 3m (10ft) but three years later, the original plants began to die out, leaving behind young suckers to replace them. Today only one of the original plants remains but a whole new generation of suckers has been allowed to colonize the gravel. They are dug up when they stray too far.

Whereas the bamboo and the viburnum cast deep shade, the loftiness of the aralias allowed us to grow a carpet of groundcover under their limbs. Sweeping under them in the gravel is a large grouping of alchemilla that has gradually migrated and become informal. This clump-forming perennial is tough yet beautiful, best used *en masse* where space allows it to develop its character. The plants that originally made up this grouping were all split from just six good specimens that allowed us enough offshoots to produce the informal drift needed to pull all the other elements together.

The biennial plants of *Angelica archangelica* that have been allowed to seed here in the shade are more haphazard in their lifestyle, seeding freely after they flower, the original plants dying out. This is a two to three year cycle and the seedlings are easy to hand pull, so we choose where they emerge, and the planting is never the same from one year to the next. Angelica is always lusher in the shade – a darker, better green, and a wonderful plant to let seed if there is room. Another migratory element that likes the cool is the Welsh poppy (*Meconopsis cambrica*), which was thrown down originally as seed into the gravel and now moves around wherever there is space. This short-lived perennial is thoroughly reliable and one of those accommodating plants that never takes up room and is quite content to find a small corner. Its flowers are a rich golden yellow, as welcome in the shade as in sunshine.

THE WATER

Not long after arriving at Home Farm the paddock in front of the house flooded. Immediately, the land was transformed, the reflections of the lonely trees on the boundary crept towards the house, the sky was drawn to the earth and the property was given a focus. The water receded in a matter of days but its image remained, a potent reminder that one day we would have to create a pond there.

Each year that passed moved us closer to a decision – a decision that was not easy to make because once we cut into the paddock, it would be changed for ever. Although there was no sign that there had ever been a pond at the front of the property, it felt as if this was the right place for one to be. We spent hours looking at where it would lie in the land and went to local ponds for inspiration. This pond would have to feel as natural as possible with blurred margins, tall reeds and habitats for wildlife. It would need to be well seated into the landscape, to appear as if it had always been there.

In the autumn of 1999, the long grass was cut so that we could see the lie of the land. The surface area was marked out with canes. We took the first impression of how big it should be and doubled it in size, taking inspiration from water in Japanese gardens that often covers as much as two-thirds of the available space. It was imperative that it felt like a significant mass that would encompass the whole of the view from the front of the house. The surface area of water always appears to shrink once it is colonized by plants. They smudge the margins and a good third of its surface, reducing the reflective value.

Our aim was to create a wildlife pond that was as natural as possible. Puddling is the traditional method used to create ponds. Livestock would be driven over a pure clay depression in wet weather to break down the soil structure and create an impervious skin to hold water. Initially we had wanted to try this method ourselves but test holes revealed that the clay soil had layers of silt that would make this less effective. We decided, therefore, to err on the side of caution and to line the pond with a PVC membrane to ensure that the water level could be maintained.

The diggers took about a week to excavate the hole and the paddock was transformed into a sea of mud, the spoil being spread out on to the remaining land. The hole itself was 1m (3ft) deep in the centre. The sides were steeply sloped where we did not want plants to colonize, to maintain views through the reeds and across the water. Marginal shelves at 30cm (12in) below the surface of the water were left where we did want water plants to grow. They were irregular in shape and would give the water line its definition, softening the boundary of water and meadow.

Once it was opened up, the hole was 'blinded off' with sand to create a soft foundation for the liner and to seal in any sharp stones. A fabric membrane was then put in place for further protection and the unwieldy liner pulled into place. The liner itself weighed 1H tons and had to be pulled out with a tractor and ropes. It unfolded like a vast black sail to cover the excavation but was soon held in place with 10cm (4in) of soil that was pushed over on to the edges to protect it from ultraviolet light and to create a planting depth for the marginal plants.

The water from a bore hole dug nearby filled the pond slowly over sixty days. (As long as no more than twenty cubic metres are extracted in one day, it is legitimate to extract ground water for domestic purposes.) Each day the reflections grew larger until when brimful, the reflective expanse was complete. It was only then that the garden really came together for the first time. From nearly every point on the property you were aware of its presence, whether it was glimpsed from up on the bank in the old orchard or through the trunks of the limes. From the front of the house the new expanse of water caught the light, night or day, and, as you moved around it, the garden and buildings were caught in a new series of reflections. For the first time the garden had an anchor. The pond was a resolution.

It was vital that the absolute flatness of the water did not feel perched in its new setting. When the surrounding land dried in early spring, it was re-contoured so that the

The paddock as seen from the front terrace, before work started on the new pond.

The pond excavations in November 1999: the diggers took a week to excavate the hole.

Drawing out the polythene liner over a blinded base of sand, to stop stones puncturing the liner.

Constructing the jetty. The pond is around 1m (3ft) deep at the centre.

water appeared to be held in a natural depression, the spoil following the gentle curves of the land. For the new contours to feel generous and in place, we examined how the land lay in the surrounding fields and we re-shaped with this greater landscape in mind.

The rough ground was harrowed and then planted with several small groups of *Alnus cordata* so that the pond was linked to the hedgerows and to Tom's Wood. These were, in the main, kept away from the water so that it remained free of leaves in the autumn. The alnus, though growing in the dry ground, would have a connotation of moisture about them with their light-reflecting leaves and spring catkins. *Salix daphnoides* 'Aglaia' and *S.d.* 'Oxford Violet' were planted in drifts around the perimeter to extend the watery feel into the land around the pond and to conceal it in parts so that, in time, a sense of mystery would develop. Once established, they would be coppiced to the ground every third year to bring out the violet stem colour and to prevent them from becoming overpowering.

In mid-spring, the ground was raked to a fine tilth and a wild-flower meadow mix sown on the re-contoured ground. The meadow was allowed to grow long to encourage wildlife; a mown path picking its way to a jetty and on to Tom's Wood. The planting of the pond itself was an event that saw us in waders and wet suits, plunging into the cold mud with the small plants. We left it until the weather had warmed in late spring so that the new water plants would be in strong growth and ready to establish in their new home. It was hard to imagine at that point that anything would come of it but in a matter of days, new spears of growth were pushing through the water.

All the plants are British natives, planted specifically to encourage wildlife. Norfolk reed, yellow flag iris (*Iris pseudacorus*) and flowering rush (*Butomus umbellatus*) are used as tall verticals around the perimeter. They were massed in large groups, one merging into the next so that the planting felt as if it had arrived by itself. The marginal beds around the jetty extend almost to its end so that it recedes into the reeds and you can walk along it and run your hands through the stems of the plants.

The marginal shelves became home to a large number of aquatic plants that took advantage of the gradient. The irises grow in several inches of water, while the king cup (*Caltha palustris*) and water mint (*Mentha aquatica*) live on the very margin between water and land. Purple loosetrife (*Lythrum salicaria*), meadowsweet (*Filipendula ulmaria*) and ragged robin (*Lychnis flos-cuculi*) occupy the marshy areas that developed around the perimeter at the extent of the liner.

In the water itself the white water lilies (*Nymphaea alba*) were contained in concrete inspection sections bought from the builder's yard, which we sat on the pond bottom. They were planted in subsoil rather than topsoil to contain their vigour (as were the plants in the marginal shelf), as each plant can cover several metres. In a balanced pond, there should be no more, and preferably no less, than one third of the water's surface exposed to the sun, otherwise the pond can suffer from algal bloom. The lilies, as well as being extremely beautiful, are useful for shading the water in the summer.

The water itself was stocked with a selection of non-invasive oxygenating weeds that would maintain the equilibrium of the water and prevent it from stagnating. We introduced water crowfoot (*Ranunculus aquatilis*), for its fine feathery growth and little white flowers that are held just above the water's surface in the spring, plus hornwort (*Ceratophyllum demersum*) and water violet (*Hottonia palustris*). Every attempt was made to avoid introducing Canadian pond weed (*Elodea*), which can take over a pond in a season.

We were advised by the ecologist from Severn Trent Water (which had helped us fund the pond as an environmental project), not to introduce any wildlife, as it is possible to carry disease from one location to the next. It would arrive by itself as larvae and eggs on plants and on the feet of wild fowl. He was quite right and each day saw a new phase of this evolution. Frog and toad spawn arrived within three weeks of filling the pond, while May Day saw the whole surface of the pond swarming with mayflies. Dragonflies, water beetles and a host of new birds have also been attracted to the area. As Frances said when she phoned to update me on the eighth water lily to come into flower: 'I am gobsmacked by the pond, Dan. I walk around it at least three times a day and I cannot think how we managed without it.'

WEEDING

It was high summer when we first set eyes on Home Farm and the land was wild and unkempt. Long grass stood thick and tall in the field, marking each flurry of wind in a little eddy of disturbance. Creeping thistle stood shoulder high, sending plumes of seed up and away on the same breeze. Elders had leapfrogged out of the woodland and taken over the old vegetable garden and even the dense bramble was white with flowering bindweed. There was a raw beauty to it and an undeniable romance, but there was also no way that we could garden here without first asserting a degree of control.

Over the time that has elapsed during the making of the garden, the land has had to be taken in hand in parts or simply steered in others for us to be able to grow what we favour. This is as true where the garden is 'cultivated' with garden plants as it is where we are 'cultivating' the wild areas. The brambles, for instance, have to be pulled from the woodland or they would smother the wild flowers there.

A 'weed' can come in any size and can take any form. It can be wild or cultivated. What separates it is its vigour. In the shaded garden to the back of the house, there has been an annual battle to control the *Galium odoratum* that, despite its demure behaviour on the competitive conditions of a woodland floor, has rampaged in the rich soil, choking and congesting all but the most vigorous of its companions. At the front of the house, in the sunshine of the grass garden, *Verbascum chaixii* 'Album' has seeded itself in its millions and although it is cut now as soon as the flowers fade and before it seeds, the maxim 'one year's seed is seven years' weed', has a certain resonance.

Galium odoratum is ideal groundcover amongst plants that will not be overwhelmed by its creeping habit. It is important to find a suitable partner such as ferns which will rise above its vigorous, weed-suppressing growth.

A plant left to seed can reproduce itself thousands of times in a single generation, which is why weeding is high on the maintenance agenda. Although the garden may look as if it has been left to fend for itself, the 'look' is a contrivance that belies the vigilant eye needed to maintain order. This is true for both wild and cultivated thugs which, left to their own devices, would soon upset the balance.

Discipline begins with a clean slate, so that new plants introduced are given a head start and a chance to get established. The tangle at the rear of the house took the best part of a year to control. The roots of bindweed went down an astonishing 2.5m (8ft) or more into the soil when the bank was excavated, so there would have been absolutely no point in beginning any new planting until it was eradicated. Even now there is a patch that comes back to haunt us at the end of the summer. By the time it is in evidence, it has

Alchemilla mollis seeds freely into the gravel but seedlings can easily be pulled where they are not needed, when they are small.

The summer cut-back will often reveal weeds in hiding. Disturbed ground can be mulched to prevent further germination.

already sent out another season's crop of white roots into the root-balls of the Scotch briars, where it is all but impossible to get to it.

The clean start is the point at which the organic argument is compromised in the garden. Where we can, the soil is left fallow for a year under black plastic or old carpet. The exclusion of light will kill all but the most persistent of weeds such as bindweed. But time is not always on our side and if there are pernicious weeds in the ground such as couch grass, ground elder or creeping thistle – plants that cannot be dug out or turned in – then we resort to glyphosate. This is a systemic herbicide which, when applied to vigorous young growth, will travel into the system of the plant and kill it from within. It is rendered inert when it touches the soil and is safe to use near water.

In the wild, unless the ground has been severely damaged or shade is so dense that it limits growth, the soil will be colonized by plants. This is what we try to emulate in the garden where the sheer density of foliage means that 'weeds' have to fight to make their presence felt. The best groundcover plants, like *Symphytum ibericum*, retain their leaves in winter and will close over in time to form colonies that repel intruders, but the greater majority of perennials die away at some point or open out above soil level, which is when invaders take their chance to set up base.

Mulching amongst plants saves hours of weeding. It is an annual process that should take place at the end of the winter once the garden is cleared. Thanks to mulching, we spend about one day a month weeding all the cultivated areas in the garden. On bare, unprotected ground it would be more like one day a week.

Little and often is the secret to successful domination. First and foremost, you will not get bored, and second, no weed will get a chance to get a hold, or worse still, seed. Vigilance is everything where weeds are concerned as they are opportunists. Anything perennial that does get a hold should be marked with a stick and dug out in the winter. Canes can be put in for bindweed to climb up, so that it can be hand-painted with a glyphosate paste, made up with wallpaper paste. Composites (dandelions, groundsel, ragwort, etc) should always be removed once they are pulled, as they have an uncanny ability to run to seed, even in their dying moments. It is always worth making a second tour of inspection and parting foliage – weeds are masters of disguise.

'Weed' control out in the wild parts of the garden is done with a bolder hand. The brambles are slashed to about 30cm (12in) and then pulled where they get out of control and if the ground is friable. Where they have got more of a purchase, they are levered out with a pick. Nettles hate to be cut back regularly, although where they are not in the way, we leave them for the butterflies. The meadows – another man-made environment – are kept in balance by removing the thatch at the end of the season so that the fertility is kept low. In these conditions the grasses grow less rampantly. When the meadows are flowering they are carefully patrolled for dock and creeping thistle, both of which are pulled so that they cannot seed. There is no intention of repeating the scene that greeted us on the very first day in high summer, but there is every intention of emulating the aesthetic.

The small meadow alongside the ridge-and-furrow fields was sown on to redistributed subsoil from the building works. We regularly have to pull creeping thistle and dock to prevent them taking over. Although these too are wild plants, they are classed as weeds in the meadow, where they would rapidly take over.

JULY

FOLIAGE

The land around Home Farm is rich and plump and fecund, a proliferation of greens that sweeps up to and over the buildings and continues off into the distance as far as the eye can see. Even when the leaves are gone and the trees and hedges stand stark, there is always a verdant feel that underpins the atmosphere. Rich pasture, thick hedgerows and dense woodland are strong influences and we have had to respect this proliferation for the boundaries between the two worlds to blur.

Crocosmia 'Lucifer' in the Barn Garden.

Cercis canadensis 'Forest Pansy' (top) forms a low shrub in dappled shade in the Woodland Garden. *Trifolium repens* 'Purpuracsens Quadrifolium' (above) is used as a dark foil groundcover in the Barn Garden. It will always colour darker where there is more light and will look pale and 'weedy' in shade.

The fusion between the wild and the tamed was relatively easy to master once we gained the confidence to wrap all the planted areas with ribbons of native plants. These plants have a quiet appeal; they are soft and unconfrontational. Nothing is jagged or brightly coloured, and what colour there is appears peppered and ephemeral. When it comes *en masse*, as with the bluebells and the blackthorn in spring, it is there for one glorious fleeting moment and then gone.

These are important markers for the way in which the garden has been planned. Choosing the right foliage for each garden is the key to its feeling of ease, as it underpins the mood and acts as the foil on which the detail can be embroidered. The floral elements of the garden are the bonus; the sparkle comes and goes but the constant green provides the key.

The Woodland Garden at the rear of the house has the very obvious influences of the adjoining wood. It is dark with ivy and light with larch and young oak in the spring but it is a constant presence that has demanded that anything placed near it feels part of it. Too many flowers would have jarred, too much colour would have looked uncomfortably out of place.

The bones of this garden have been fleshed out with a voluminous layering of leaves that are used for contrast, form and texture. Early on in the year when the planting erupts, the foliage is so rich and lush that there is little need for floral embellishment. Giant palm-shaped leaves of the ornamental rhubarb (*Rheum*) contrast with filigree ferns and thalictrum. Lime-green astrantia is almost luminous under the young copper leaves of *Amelanchier*.

Dark foliage has been used in this garden to add a sense of depth, like pools of shade. Two large groups of copper-leaved hazels add the main weight and against them we have been free to play with plants that have a sense of lightness. *Epilobium angustifolium* var. *album*, which is interplanted through the tellima, is pale early on in the year when its delicate apple green leaves unfurl and then brilliant white in flower against the substantial dark

The Woodland Garden from the bedroom windows at the back of the house. Over the seasons, this riot of growth changes weekly. The planting is treated like a canvas and we are always working on the whole composition to keep it in balance.

background of the hazels. *Cotinus coggygria* 'Royal Purple' adds weight in the garden, though the plants have been dissipated rather than clumped together for fear that the dark foliage would weigh too heavily.

As contrast, and to add a shimmer, is the silver of *Sorbus aria* 'Lutescens', which is glorious for two weeks in spring but then tones down for the remainder of the summer. The dusky silver *Rosa glauca* is planted in large groups to maintain the lightness and as a foil to a mass of pink-flowered persicaria, which need the neutrality of foliage to anchor them. There is also a proliferation of foliage with a good proportion of brown in the green – *Cornus alba* 'Kesselringii', *Lysimachia ciliata* 'Firecracker' and the young foliage of *Aruncus sylvestris*. Coppery brown is wonderfully neutral: it blends with the dark hazels and adds depth to the lighter silvers and to greens that verge on being yellow.

Lupinus arboreus.

Cotinus coggygria 'Royal Purple'.

The pale, acidic greens of *Cornus alba* 'Aurea', the golden hop (*Humulus lupulus* 'Aureus') and *Milium effusum* 'Aureum' are kept to the lower, shaded areas of this garden and are used to add a feeling of artificial sunlight. Even on a dull day, they lift the planting and allow us to use conventional greens more freely without them becoming monotonous.

The cardoons were a good example of a plant that failed to fit into the Woodland Garden. They were brought up from the previous London garden and soon began to look out of place where they were planted initially. Although the architecture of the foliage was magnificent, it was altogether too strong, its silver needing a sunnier atmosphere to make it work. The cardoons also needed to be anchored to the buildings for them to register as an obvious introduction. They were found a place close to the house on the edges of the vegetable garden and there they have been free to reign.

At the front of the property the sunshine and the sense of enclosure up on the terrace allowed more freedom. Other exotics such as *Melianthus major* look appropriate by the front door and the great plantings of silvery *Elaeagnus* 'Quicksilver' have meant that the whole atmosphere here has been embued with light. The foliage of the bronze fennel and the yews and underplantings of dark-leaved *Viola labradorica* look all the darker for the silver. The copper-leaved form of the native elder (*Sambucus nigra* 'Guincho Purple') has also been used here up by the buildings to add weight and to refer to the occasional copper beech that pushes through the copse above the old orchard. The self-sown ox-eye daisies are the native ribbon here, infiltrating all the gravel areas, scattering the hard surfaces with a calm green for eleven months of the year and frothing white when their moment comes.

CALM

Each of the gardens that surrounds the property has its own particular temperament. The mood of each of these places is always underpinned by the colour that has been used there and although it may not be the first thing that you notice, it is the essential infusion.

We have had many, many conversations about the colour in the garden and over the years have made drastic changes to get it just right. As the planting has become more confident, the colour palette, too, has been identified and we now have a better idea of what works and where it is most appropriate.

The majority of the garden is planted with a subtlety that allows the eye free movement from one point to the next and then out into the landscape. There is a palette for each area, in which the theme is mapped out in large tonal swathes. Within it there are no frantic juxtapositions to distract the eye, the detail is much as it would be in a meadow, as a peppering for contrast. Within the overall picture the detail is energizing – treasure that you stumble upon if you decide to pause.

It has taken time to get the colour right. Time to let the plants perform and then time to see how we feel about the mood with which they infuse each area. This has sometimes meant that we have had to make radical and unsentimental changes. The *Clematis* 'Perle d'Azur' that grew more heartily that any other I had seen was a good example. It smothered the front of the house in high summer with a shimmer of blue that you could see from across the fields. It was spectacular but during one of our many conversations about the garden, Frances declared that it would have to go. She had seen beyond its horticultural success and realized that the front of the house should be quieter, that the stone of the walls and the setting demanded that the subtlety of what was already there was not overwhelmed. Losing it was a wrench but she was right. It was dug up. A home was found for it elsewhere and we replaced it with the dusky plum-flowered *Clematis viticella* 'Purpurea Plena Elegans'.

The purple-mauve of the new clematis is almost hidden among the purple-leaved grape on the front wall and although the colour is less obvious, it is ultimately more interesting. It is part of a palette that has infused the planting with a quiet drama that you can look into but can also look beyond, with ease. Colour here is applied with a light hand, and is rarely used in blocks. Dark ruby *Astrantia major* 'Hadspen Blood' drifts through faded purple *Lavatera* 'Burgundy Wine' while liquorice-flowered *Papaver somniferum* adds weight to the reds. The metallic mauve of *Allium cristophii* adds a sparkle amongst the plain catmint (*Nepeta cataria*) and tiny flecks of stone red *Lathyrus rotundifolius* add a dash of chilli-like spice.

The colours already found in the environment are the key to the palette and we have tapped into the mood of each area to provide a continuous narrative as you walk around the garden. In the Woodland Garden, the cool greens are injected with colour that is restful and clean. Down in the shade of the house, the lime-green of the *Alchemilla mollis* provides a base note that lifts what could otherwise be a sombre corner. It is enlivened with blue *Brunnera macrophylla* and *Clematis alpina* 'Frances Rivis' for the early part of the season and self-sown *Meconopsis cambrica* for its pure buttercup yellow. Blues are best in shade where they can pulse and hover; sun tends to overwhelm them. This is one of the few places where yellow is used in the garden as it can easily dominate but here, in moderation, the meconopsis can fool you into thinking that the light is dappled.

The cool atmosphere is heightened with cream honeysuckle *Lonicera periclymenum* 'Graham Thomas' and smatterings of white that lift the darkness and add sparkle. Whites are like light reflected in an eye – it is the reflection that brings the eye to life. The arching bramble *Rubus* 'Benenden' will do just this on the dark bank in May when it is scattered with its pure-white single flowers. Starry *Galium odoratum* picks up the white at its feet and whites in all their various shades of purity are essential highlights throughout the rest of the year, culminating in the tapering spires of *Persicaria amplexicaulis* 'Alba'.

Used in larger volumes, the whites tend to be kept apart so that one will not muddy the next, as the degrees of white are all so different. *Rosa* 'Nevada' and *Epilobium angustifolium var.* 'Album' are good companions, however, and look all the whiter for their dark background of holly and corylus. *Aruncus sylvestris*, though, is a rich dark cream and has been linked to the yellow of *Cornus alba* 'Aurea'. *Crambe cordifolia* is a pure dazzling white that remains light and never dominant, as its cage of flowers soars overhead. This is a powerful plant that has a brief but glorious moment of flower. You need enough room for it or it will lean on its neighbours, and you have to be prepared for it suddenly to sulk. It's my belief that earwigs get into the crowns to hollow them out, so we grow four plants staggered across the garden and divide one each year to keep them in good condition.

The pinks in this garden are soft and clear when used *en masse* and stronger when used as injections of energy. The pink-flowered *Persicaria amplexicaulis* 'Rosea' is used in a great drift in the sunniest part of the garden. It would not be as interesting if it was not broken by the strong carmine of the echinacea and the occasional flecking that the bloody cranesbill (*Geranium sanguineum*) injects where it has been allowed to self-seed. This planting is always at its best in high summer and although the harsh light can bleach out the colour at noon, it is always there at the beginning and end of the day.

Dark saturated colours are also used to add depth and provide a quiet but profound punch. *Geranium psilostemon* is wonderful where it hovers in the shade by the yew shelter, its magenta flowers all the better for a dark background. The ruby-red *Cirsium rivulare* 'Atropurpureum' and the royal blue of *Aconitum* 'Sparks Variety' add a jewel-like intensity to the planting that prevents the softness here from ever becoming precious. Dark colours always need a lift and tiny flecks of red and orange are used to invigorate them. The soft apricot *Papaver rupifragum* adds levity to the darkness of the bronze fennel and occasional

The short-lived perennial *Papaver rupifragum* amongst bronze fennel, *Foeniculum vulgare* 'Purpureum'.

Camassia leichtlinii 'Alba' (top).
Nectaroscordum siculum subsp. *bulgaricum* (above).
Clematis viticella 'Purpurea Plena Elegans' with *Vitis vinifera* 'Purpurea' (opposite).

clumps of *Crocosmia* 'Lucifer' enliven the dark mass of copper-leaved *Cornus alba* 'Kesselringii'.

Although it is always evident, strong colour has been used with restraint. When it has been used in concentration, it has been revealed as a surprise and indulged in its own space, as in the Barn Garden. In the areas that are open and connected to the landscape, the colour is more low key.

The colour at the front of the house is almost the opposite of the heat and intensity in the Barn Garden. It is more about the barn walls and the meadow land beyond. It is colour that is discreet, muted and full of subtlety. As with many of the plantings, there has always been one plant that picks up a particular colour. It is the *Digitalis ferruginea* in the Barn Garden that so perfectly makes the connection between the rusty walls and the fire of many of the plants there. Similarly, the *Nectaroscordum siculum* are the inspiration in the planting at the front. When in flower, the soft green bells are overlaid with the colours of stone, plums and storm clouds. They are subdued yet potent. When the plants dry, they fade to buff and parchment white, doing so in tandem with the blonding of the summer meadows beyond.

Elements of the colour found in these plants have been exploited in the planting, pale grasses forming the link to the meadow land beyond. The bright green of cut grass is kept well away from this area. It is altogether too overwhelming in its intensity. Large drifts of colour are used here, *Salvia verticillata* 'Purple Rain' forming the base note, along with the muted tones of *Acaena microphylla* 'Kupferteppich'. The freedom with which they cover the space is reminiscent of the dark wooded hills in the background and the fields when they are ploughed brown. Plum-coloured *Sedum telephium* 'Matrona', chocolate-leaved *Aster lateriflorus* 'Horizontalis' and dark-thimbled *Sanguisorba officinalis* 'Tanna' puncture the expanse of violet and bronze, and self-sown poppies are allowed to seed into this otherwise muted scene.

The Barn Garden in July shortly after the eremurus have gone over. Stems of *Digitalis ferruginea* replace their strong vertical accents amongst the softness of the grasses.

HEAT

What is particular about the Barn Garden is the quality of light and the feeling of open airiness. The rising sun sets the rusty barn wall alight and in the heat of the day the creamy cobbles bounce light back from underfoot. The combination of stone and the tawny meadow grasses were the main inspiration for this garden, and it is in complete contrast to the cool atmosphere of the back garden.

The Barn Garden has been enclosed by replacing the fallen wall with a yew hedge. There is nothing quite like the neutral matt green of yew, with its tightly woven texture and darkness, throwing the garden inside into relief. In certain light it looks almost black, the dense opposite to the light-filled *Stipa gigantea* and incandescent colour within.

The hedge partially screens the planting from the outside so that, as you enter through the small gap in the hedge, the impact is maximized. The Fire Garden is the alternative name for this enclosure. At its peak in mid-summer, its colours are so intensely energizing that you feel almost a sense of loss when you leave the garden. It is only then that you realize your pulse has been racing.

The yew, the rusty walls and the cobbles set the tone in the garden. The ground plane of dark clovers (*Trifolium*), *Euphorbia dulcis* 'Chameleon' and *Knautia macedonica* provide the underpinning and gravity for the injections of energetic colour that come through later in pulses and waves. The golden stems of *Stipa gigantea* are lifted by the dark undercurrent that gives the vermilion of the *Crocosmia* 'Lucifer' the background it needs to glow. Foliage infused with brown, copper and rust is chosen in preference to green so that, as a whole, the garden's tone is bronze.

There are two clovers in the garden, *Trifolium repens* 'Purpurascens Quadrifolium' being the stronger and browner of the two. This is one of the plants that Frances originally bought from Beth Chatto and it has remained a favourite, the hard living and generous

light helping to maximize its colour. It has taken over the cobbles in places and we leave it to be trampled underfoot to soften the little pathways through the garden. *Trifolium repens* 'Wheatfen' is the second of the two, more ruby-red in leaf but unfortunately prone to slug attack. It has to be divided every two years to keep stocks from dwindling: a small price for the contrast that it gives to the apricot *Potentilla* x *tonguei*.

There are other coppery tones early on in the season. The young growth on *Rosa* 'Scharlachglut' is almost as good as the crimson flowers that follow later and the little creeping *Euphorbia cyparissias* 'Clarice Howard' is a dark undercurrent early on until it erupts in a small eddy of lime-green flowers during May. The positive–negative contrast when it comes into contact with the vermilion of the *Potentilla* 'Gibson's Scarlet' is essential. It is important to let things sing and vibrate occasionally, otherwise the whole picture loses a vital energy.

Contrast is not always as obviously energetic. The geranium red of *Rosa moyesii* is made pinker by the under-planting of the poppy, *Papaver* 'Orange King'; the orange of the poppy itself brighter for the dark tomato-red of *Euphorbia griffithii* 'Dixter' nearby.

The garden was deliberately planted with a reduced plant list, the key plants – in this case the roses – going in first as anchor points. Certain plants such *Stipa gigantea* are planted in a broad crescent across the garden. Then there are thirty plants of *Calamagrostis brachytricha*, a later-flowering grass, drifted through the centre and large numbers of rust-red daylily *Hemerocallis* 'Stafford' and *Potentilla* 'Gibson's Scarlet' punctuate the space. Among the large drifts there is still room for some occasional jewels that can be found on closer observation, but these are always linked and rarely in isolation.

Colour comes in waves, starting with the eschscholtzia and the copper-toned stipas. The eremurus score vertical lines in burnt orange and clear yellow at this point. There are two varieties here, the burnt orange of 'Cleopatra' a necessary contrast to yellow 'Moneymaker'. They form

Eschscholtzia californica 'Orange King' (above). *Rosa* 'Scharlachglut' (opposite). *Digitalis ferruginea* (previous pages) picking out the rust colour of ironstone wall in the Barn Garden. Orange *Eschscholtzia californica* and *Stipa gigantea* in the background continue the feeling of warmth.

E. x *isabellinus* 'Cleopatra'. Eremurus tend to become overcrowded after five years or so and need dividing.

Hemerocallis 'Stafford' with *Potentilla* 'Gibson's Scarlet' at its base, and *Stipa gigantea* and *Monarda* 'Cambridge Scarlet' in the background.

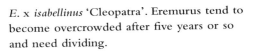

an upright motion that is picked up with the rust spires of *Digitalis ferruginea* and followed through with the orange glow of the later-flowering *Kniphofia* 'Prince Igor'. These verticals are used like lighted torches in the garden to illuminate the grasses and the darker tones underneath.

The brilliant orange flowers of *Eschscholtzia californica* 'Aurantiaca Orange King' lift the garden from the slow burn of spring to the roar of high summer. The orange is so saturated and so intensely satiny that it is a yardstick against which other hues are measured. These poppies also act as a marker of summer, the first flower unscrolling is never, ever a disappointment.

When the garden was first planted, the eschscholtzias were sown from seed in late March in the gaps, to give the garden a lived-in feel in the first season. As the garden has evolved, they have been allowed to seed about, a ruthless cull reducing numbers in late May so that they do not smother other precious plants or become overwhelming. But their overall presence is a unifying element in the garden and helps to hold the planting together.

Swatches of colour are used elsewhere to take your eye into corners or to draw you through the garden. The darkness of *Knautia macedonica* pinpricks the garden with ruby red and *Rosa* 'Scharlachglut' is underplanted with a solid block of *Monarda* 'Cambridge

Eremurus 'Moneymaker' and *E.* x *isabellinus* 'Cleopatra' need open ground to grow in before flowering but their leaves will wither away in July once they have replenished the roots. The hole they leave behind is filled with a late-flowering grass, *Calamagrostis brachytricha*, and *Knautia macedonica*.

Scarlet' to add weight to one corner. *Paeonia* 'Scarlett O'Hara' anchors the light primrose of *Cephalaria gigantea*, the giant scabious. This plant is at its best when the stipa has unfolded and is hung with golden pollen. The paleness of this combination also has a wonderful moment when the stipa is wetted by rain and turns from gold to hot cinnamon.

The flowering of *Kniphofia* 'Prince Igor' marks the turning point of summer that sees the hips of the roses infused with amber and the *Calamagrostis brachytricha* turning a thunderous purple grey. The strong deep red of *Dahlia* 'Bishop of Llandaff' is more strident now that the light has changed; the dark rusts and brown red of *Helianthus* 'Velvet Queen' a heavy presence amongst the rose hips. The garden takes on a luminosity that replaces the tension of high summer. It begins to return to its earth tones once again in preparation for the softness of the autumn and the bleaching monochrome of winter.

AUGUST

MOVEMENT

Movement is one of the unsung glories of a garden. Never static, the ebb and flow of the seasons will see each and every corner altered in the cycle of a year. There is a still stiffness to winter. The garden will twitch with growth in the early spring, then surge, melt and roll in summer as each space is filled to bursting. It will hold itself high, as it is doing at the moment, but recede again, to rest in winter.

Silver poplars (*Populus alba*) are rapid-growing expansive trees that are at their best when the leaves are lifted by wind to reveal their silver undersides.

The Grass Garden in the first year after planting was dominated by *Stipa tenuissima*. Over the years, as the planting has established, this sun-loving grass has colonized at the outer edges of the planting where it is able to be at its most mobile. The yew forms have yet to establish their weight and structure although they are already adding a solid contrast to the mobility of the grasses.

Although it is all too easy to have your head down in the tasks of running a garden, it is important to stop, sit and look. I will often take time when the feeling of frenzy has subsided to sit on one of the perches that have been placed at strategic points in the garden. Placed low down in the Barn Garden are two stones we found that must have once been the tops of 'mushrooms' used to prevent rodents getting into a granary. Sitting on them, low down among the foliage, you get a child's perspective of the garden. Once you are completely surrounded by the plants, you are fully aware of the movement.

The grasses are at their best now, rising up to form a veil that casts its net across much of the garden. The dry dustiness is infused with the rustle of stems and, with the whisper of their flowering heads, comes the addition of motion. It is as if there is a dance being

performed in the garden, each plant contributing its own specific movement.

The *Stipa gigantea* has long flowering stems that emerge from a tight evergreen clump of foliage at ground level. The plumes act like sails on these long stems, catching the breeze and causing the whole plant to swagger when the wind blows. Earlier on in the summer, the flowering awns, golden with pollen, twitch and gyrate on their hinges like trapeze artists balancing in space. *Calamagrostis brachytricha* captures a different movement altogether, its wider leaves are more voluminous and mobile. They are planted in a drift across the middle of the garden that captures each eddy, charting the passage of the wind.

At the front of the house, *Stipa tenuissima* has been used to take advantage of the breeze that moves across the garden from the west. The grasses form a low ground plane that, from the moment they flower in early summer, is in constant flux. Even at those times when you are not aware of there being any breeze, the stipas will indicate the air-flow. The planting appears almost aquatic, as if the grasses are weeds on the bottom of a rock pool that are being pulled and pushed by underwater currents. When the wind is blowing hard, they are bent over in its direction or if it is gusting, tossed back and forth.

The planting in the Lime Enclosure has a subtle drama that comes to light when the garden is at its most mobile. If you use the analogy of choreography, you would say that the yew forms add to the feeling of motion by their very stillness. They are the immovable

Calamagrostis brachytricha in flower in late summer with *Stipa gigantea* in the background.

rocks that are the contrast to the stipas. You would hardly notice the stillness of the yew were it not for the grasses; the motion in the grasses would be less marked if not for the yew. Two large pools of *Ruta graveolens* 'Jackman's Blue' also act as an anchor in this planting; without them the mobility of everything else could be bothersome.

Rising out of the ground plane of stipas are punctuations of dierama, which, when they are flowering, arch over on long wiry stems that bow and arc in the breeze. They are followed on by two forms of molinia which stride out of the Lime Enclosure into the planting beyond, as if they are making a move on the landscape. *Molinia caerulea* subsp. *arundinacea* 'Karl Foerster' is the smaller of the two, growing tall and upright to about shoulder-height from a deciduous clump of growth that remains low. Its free stems are like high-tensile wire rising bolt upright so the motion is stiff but fluid. The cultivar 'Windspiel' is even more dramatic, growing to 2m (6½ft) and arching over at the top. This is a plant that needs space in which to perform. We moved it out into the drift of salvias in front of the barn doors so that you could really experience the tossing and swaying of its plumes in late summer. These plants demand low planting around them. Their basal growth dislikes competition and their heads need a clear stage for the performance at the end of summer.

The reeds in the pond benefit from the grand sweep in which they are planted. Working as a community to map the wind across the garden, they take your eye out into the greater landscape. From the jetty on the pond you can look along the length of the water. Some days this is as still and serene as glass but when the wind blows it is blurred, your eye travelling across the reeds and out again, over the silver poplars planted to the east of the garden. Their upturned leaves, ruffled and lifted by the westerly wind, are exposed to the light. It is now in high summer that they are at their best, the shoals of silver leaves turning this way and that. Magic in motion.

CLIMBERS

The walls at Home Farm are one of the most beautiful attributes of the property. A rich rust in colour, the ironstone has been colonized over the years by a textile of lichens. The stone flares in warm evening sunlight and creates a spectacle. It would be entirely inappropriate to cover these walls so climbers have been kept to a minimum in the garden. Where we have used them, it has been to hide the Victorian brick extension at the rear of the house. There, they have taken the profusion of the garden up on to the walls so that the building is softened and drawn into its welcoming greenery. Climbers have also been used at the front of the house to romp loosely over the walls to the same end. In places, they have been planted to take interest skyward into the trees.

Allowed to grow soft and informal, climbers blur hard edges and give the garden a sense of abandonment. From relatively little space at ground level, they will create voluminous growth above ground – and this is how they have been used at the front of the house. Here the beds are small (to maximize room on the terrace) but there is a feeling of profusion because the walls are burgeoning, planted with two *Rosa* 'Madame Alfred Carrière', one on each side of the doorway. They romped up to the eaves in two years and have to be trained hard into a fan each winter to keep them within bounds. Their winter formality, however, is just as interesting as the profusion of summer growth and a welcome contrast.

'Madame Alfred Carrière' is a good rose. It is strong and recurrent, its main flush of loose-petalled delicately scented cream flowers followed by intermittent blooms for the whole of the summer. Its limbs are strong so the frame of the rose has been used as a support for *Vitis vinifera* 'Purpurea' and the dusky double-flowered *Clematis viticella* 'Purpurea Plena Elegans'. The look is subdued but interesting, altogether different from the *Clematis* 'Perle d'Azur' that we grew here beforehand.

Walking around four sides of the house is like moving from one climate to the next. The meeting point between a west-facing wall and a north-facing one gives almost opposing conditions in which to garden. To thrive, the plants have to reflect this change: although the climbers love the sunshine at the front of the house, those that have been chosen specifically for the opposing conditions on the north-facing walls at the back are just as contented.

The informality of *Rosa multiflora* softens the front of the house (previous page). It has a brief season in flower but will go on to produce hips that last into the winter. Dark-leaved *Lonicera japonica* var. *repens* clambers through it to extend its season and provide scent around the doorway. *Jasminum officinalis* covers the remainder of the façade.

Lonicera periclymenum 'Graham Thomas' has been allowed to cover the greater majority of the rear wall. This is one of the best honeysuckles, being both strong and recurrent. It is a cream selection of the wild honeysuckle so the atmosphere it creates is soft and unconfrontational. It thrives in cool conditions and seems as happy here as in sunshine. When in full flower in mid-summer, it fills the house with scent. The remainder of the wall is colonized by two clematis, which occupy their own spaces because of their differing flowering habits. *Clematis alpina* 'Frances Rivis' flowers in early spring, its dark-blue flowers luminous in shade. It is only ever pruned immediately after flowering to keep it in bounds. Were it pruned along with most other clematis in late winter, all its flowering wood would be removed and it would be 'blinded' for a year.

Clematis 'Niobe' growing here through *Cotinus coggygria* 'Royal Purple' with *Nicotiana alata* in the background.

Lonicera periclymenum 'Graham Thomas' is a selection of the native honeysuckle. It will bloom off and on after its main season until November.

Clematis 'Bill McKenzie' occupies the remainder of the wall. Its flowers are a saturated gold that lights up the dull wall from mid-summer until late autumn, when the silvered seed heads take over for the winter. Unlike its partner, it is sheared back to a loose framework at the end of winter. Without its annual cut, it would form a great unmanageable bird's nest.

The climbers on the walls are all given a good start in life because the soil under the eaves is dry and full of rubble. A large hole is removed, two spits deep and 60cm (2ft) wide – climbers are long-term occupants that need to draw upon good resources. (When planting climbers near a tree the same principle applies, though if the tree is dense it is best to dig out the planting hole away from the drip-line and train the climber up canes into the foliage.)

Clematis viticella is one of the most delicately flowered of the summer clematis, although it is vigorous in growth and will grow to several metres after hard pruning in February. It is used on the front terrace as a partner to white-flowered buddleia, which also provides support in the summer months.

The hole is then back-filled with a mixture of compost and good topsoil, and a handful of blood, fish and bone. The climbers are planted with a decent gap between them and the wall to ensure that they have access to water, although they are watered regularly for the first year.

In the first season they will be trained on to a series of horizontal wires 30cm (12in) apart attached to the wall with rawlplugs and vine eyes. Economizing on the wiring is a mistake: the weight of a full-grown plant and the influence of wind can be considerable. Self-clinging climbers are not used against the house walls in case they damage the soft stone. Care in the early days to get the plant on to its new support will be time well spent. Left to writhe around on the ground, most climbers will of course eventually clamber skyward, but it will take longer.

Vigour is an issue with the climbers on the house. Even though the plants have been chosen for the space they have to fill, it is a time-consuming task to remove them from the gutters every year and to prevent them obliterating windows. You have to feel secure on a ladder so we only ever wire to the height we are prepared to climb. Letting plants loose into trees is another story, although vigour once again has to be taken into consideration. *Rosa filipes* 'Kiftsgate' was removed from the old apple trees after seeing it smothering several trees in the gardens at Kiftsgate. To avoid total domination, it was replaced with 'Bobbie James' and 'Wedding Day'. They illuminate the old trees in summer with a great cloud of blossom, with 'Bobbie James' taking over from the earlier flowering 'Wedding Day'.

Elsewhere in the garden, climbers are used to add a layer of interest. The golden hop (*Humulus lupulus* 'Aureus') is encouraged through *Rubus* 'Benenden', providing cover for the rubus once it has flowered and to throw light into a dark corner. Clematis are used in and over shrubs. *Clematis* 'Niobe' is trained through the dark leaves of *Cotinus coggygria* 'Royal Purple'. The saturation of colour is as rich as old velvet. Elsewhere, smaller-flowered viticella clematis are used because they have a lightness and grace that is in keeping with the naturalism of the garden. 'Viticella Rubra' clambers over the philadelphus once it is over and spots the white willow herb there with dark wine red. 'Etoile Violette' clambers over the *Rosa glauca* and, at the front, the species viticella is used to scramble up and into white buddleia. This is a personal favourite. Pruned hard in February, it comes back with a vengeance and is covered for weeks with small bells of matt purple.

DRY GARDENING

Over the years the garden at Home Farm has steadily been increasing in size. But as we burst out of one area and spilled into the next, it was not simply a case of picking up where we left off. We soon discovered that each new area had its own very specific set of conditions. The exposure of the Barn Garden, for example, could not be more different from the calm shade and ambient moisture of the garden at the rear. Plants could not be treated in the same way here when subjected to wind and baking sunshine in the summer months and cold easterlies in the winter.

Despite the differing conditions that presented themselves in each area, one of the discoveries that united the garden was that it was drier than we had expected. Despite the heavy soil, the gentle south-facing slope on which most of the garden lies means that the ground drains freely. Come the summer, much of the garden bakes dry, great fissures big enough to slip your fingers down opening up in the soil where it has not been mulched. Mulching and soil improvement have been essential and have helped, but a plant that is gasping for water is very difficult to ignore. This raised the issue once again of the right plant for the right place and it soon became clear that we would have to garden with drought very much in mind.

We try not to water where we can in the garden on principle. Water is becoming increasingly valuable and if you look to nature, it resolves the problem by adapting. Plants with large leaves that would dry like sheets in the wind confine themselves to sheltered corners or have their feet within reach of water. Where there is little water available, we use plants with leaves reduced in size or lost almost entirely in plants like broom.

Every palette of plants has been chosen to match the conditions in each area so that they will thrive for the greater part of the time without the need for constant cosseting. *Luzula sylvatica* and tiarella are happy in the dry shade, and *Verbena bonariensis* is at its best where it gets a real baking. Over the years, some plants have been moved five or six times to get the position right and many have had to be rejected altogether. Although we *will* water, we do so only at critical points, to establish the plantings in their first season or in the Vegetable Garden, to promote lush growth. In the garden, plants will always be given a good start in life but beyond that are expected to fend for themselves, as there is a lot of ground to cover and limited labour to do so.

The Barn Garden was the first area that really tested this resolve. Dry winds and baking sunshine in the summer can transform it in a matter of hours, the grasses rolling up their leaves to conserve moisture. This can be upsetting when it happens and you can feel your own stress levels rising, but come the evening when temperatures drop the leaves unroll and calm returns. *Stipa gigantea* is the most resilient of the grasses in this situation, the later-flowering *Calamagrostis brachytricha* showing stress more easily. The grasses are not the only plants that have adapted to cope with the drought. The eremurus grow away early in the year when there is plenty of moisture and wither to nothing in the summer (as they would in their native Middle East, safe below ground). The hemerocallis and the *Crocosmia* 'Lucifer' also have moisture-retaining underground organs and all have lance-shaped leaves with a reduced surface to conserve moisture.

The Barn Garden does not have the same conditions throughout, however. The top side (where the cobbles are) drains and bakes, the lower side remains more moist, and the soil is cooler in the shade of the wall. Plants that prefer more moisture are planted on the

The Lime Enclosure in August with silver drifts of *Eryngium giganteum* and white tapering *Verbascum chaixii* 'Album'. Both are prolific seeders and have to be watched. The verbascum is cut to the base as soon as the flowers fade but the eryngium are left for their winter forms and the seedlings hoed out where they are not needed in the spring.

lower side. *Euphorbia griffithii* is contented here and the heleniums have finally been found a home in which they can flourish. Coming from the prairies of America, they are used to getting their feet down into cool soil although their heads like the sunshine. The helianthus like the richer living here, as do the dahlias. Although all these differences might not be immediately obvious when looking at the garden as a whole, a certain balance has been struck, with the plants growing where they are happiest.

The driest part of the whole garden is to the front of the house alongside the drive. This was an old droving route and there is little, if any, soil to speak of – not much more than dust and shale. But this situation presents its own potential and, with careful choice, we have been able to colonize the gravel with drought lovers. The secret has been to find plants that come from similar situations and then to give them a good start by excavating

Previous pages: *Verbascum chaixii* 'Album' amongst the *Limonium latifolium* (left), which forms low but significant mounds in the Grass Garden, flowering silvery-mauve at a potential dull moment in August. *Eryngium giganteum* amongst *Stipa tenuissima* (right).

a hole twice as large as the root-ball and back-filling with decent soil. The plants are watered in and the gravel used as a mulch after planting to keep the moisture in the soil underneath.

Lavender loves this position. Growing hard suits it, and in time the bushes become gnarled and woody, and live longer as a result. The tree lupins love it too as they naturally grow by the coast in sand dunes. After introducing them initially, they have self-sown. We pull them out after three or four years when they begin to fall apart. They are short lived and look best before they reach middle age. The eldest plants are simply removed and another self-sown seedling grown in its place. They have been 'anchored' with a carpet of native ox-eye daisies that were thrown down as seed in the autumn to flower the following summer. The daisies do have to be confined to this position as they are thugs in rich soil. Self-sown bronze fennel has been encouraged and *Verbascum bombyciferum*, both of which have seeded into this free-draining medium – any seedlings that look out of place have simply been pulled.

Below the drive, the soil is better, but the position faces due south, the gentle slope soaking up the sun. This area has only ever been watered at planting time and in the first season to establish the youngsters. This is critical, particularly if planting takes place in the spring with the potential of a dry summer ahead. If the pots are dry, then they are plunged into a bucket of water until the air bubbles stop rising to the surface; after planting, each plant is watered to settle the soil around the root-ball so that contact is made between the root and its new environment. Planted in autumn, the roots will get a hold by the spring and more often than not the area will only need one good drenching in the summer to ensure the plants are not stressed. If planted in the spring, watering may need to be more frequent to help them establish.

Acaena microphylla 'Kupferteppich'.

The Thyme Garden is grown hard like the lavender. Thymes are wonderful plants for a dry position, hailing originally from the Mediterranean. The more extreme the situation, the tighter and more aromatic they become, their tiny leaves being well adapted to drought. The soil was well prepared with compost before they were planted in early spring to avoid the worst of the weather. Most Mediterranean evergreens prefer a spring planting. The cosseting at the beginning meant that within three months the young plants had grown together and covered the soil so there was no need to mulch. Excessive growth has been discouraged by growing them hard, without irrigation or feeding. They thrive on these conditions once established. Being sun lovers, where they are shaded by the Lime Enclosure, they have died out but have been replaced by *Acaena microphylla* 'Kupferteppich'.

Planting within the Lime Enclosure is also designed with drought in mind, using plants that are reminiscent of coastal areas or desert. Planted through mounds of yew and glaucous-leaved rue there is a ground plane of *Stipa tenuissima* that knits the planting together. The grass is punctured by the burnt orange form of the horned poppy (*Glaucium flavum*), which grows in nothing more than shingle by the coast. It has died out here where the living has been too good but the seedlings have a knack of finding a barren corner in which to thrive, in the dry area at the base of the yew and in the gravel of the drive. Tall *Verbascum chaixii* 'Album' and *Dierama pulcherrimum* form another layer in the planting. The verbascum is so happy here, it has to be watched so that it does not seed, but the dierama, on the other hand, has taken a while to establish and we have had to add sharp sand in the planting holes to help them to take. Once they are growing happily, they can cope with the heavy soil, though they have suffered in wet winters.

The stipa is short-lived by nature so over time the planting moves in and out of the limes and into the gravel of the drive. The oldest plants begin to flop and matt like uncombed hair after three years, and they are pulled to make way for a new generation of seedlings. They seem to actively prefer the tough living in the drive, where, in the dry conditions, they seed freely, though never in a way that presents a problem. The gaps that open when the stipas are pulled free up space for the biennial *Eryngium giganteum*, which seeds freely when it is in sunshine and is more silvered and spectacular the drier the season.

Ferula communis will need three seasons to grow from seed before it flowers. It hates disturbance, needing to send its long tap root down deep to support its 3m (10ft) flower heads.

SEPTEMBER

9

HARVEST

Over the past month, the harvested fields in the distance have brought with them a different mood. The hills are blond where they have been cut and the pasture is dry after the summer. September is one of the most beautiful months. The pale cast that has been thrown over the garden is injected with saturated colour from late-flowering plants. The dahlias are at their best and *Helianthus* 'Velvet Queen' is branched now with multiple flower heads.

Crested cobnuts on *Corylus avellana* 'Purpurea' in the Woodland Garden.

Garlic drying.

Redcurrants.

Raspberry 'Leo'.

Potato harvest.

Runner beans.

Pumpkin 'Uchiki Kuri'.

Squash 'Gemstone'.

Pumpkin 'Small Sugar'.

French beans 'Viola Cornetti' and 'Sungold'.

Both have been dead–headed to keep them producing flowers over the summer, but now they are left to have a final fling as the growing season is coming to a close.

The weather is often reliable this month so we will take the opportunity to cut the meadows. Traditional hay meadows would have been harvested by mid–summer 'when the yellow rattle rattles' and the ground put down to grazing again. Over years the removal of the hay reduces the fertility in the soil, which in turn weakens the grasses, which prefer rich soil. The wild flowers can compete when the grasses are less dominant, which is why the oldest meadows are often the most dynamic.

The meadows on the rich soil at Home Farm are problematic as the grasses tend to overwhelm the wild flowers. The little meadow behind the Barn Garden is the most successful because it was sown on to made-up ground that was no more than subsoil from the excavations at the back of the house.

The meadows are left for as long as possible so that the late–flowering knapweed (*Centaurea nigra*) and yarrow (*Achillea millefolium*) can continue to provide interest. Most of the seed of other species will have been thrown down by now and if the weather has remained dry, the new thatch of growth that will push through underneath has still to make a start. Once it has started to grow, it can make cutting a time–consuming and labour–intensive task, so we hope for dry weather for this job.

The small meadow behind the Barn Garden can take all day to clear with a strimmer, scythe and rakes. We make sure that as much of the thatch is removed as possible – almost back to bare soil – to keep the fertility low. It is taken up to the compost heap where it will be added in layers over the autumn. The land that is left behind looks shorn and naked but a month will see it green up again; it is then that you can see how the community of plants that regenerate is getting richer and more diverse each year.

Saving seed is one of the jobs in the garden that is very easily overlooked during the riot of summer, but it is well worth doing. Friends always want seed of the annual black opium poppy (*Papaver somniferum*). It seems to resent growing in the same place from one year to the next so a jarful will be saved and a handful of seed sown in a new area as soon as it is ripe. The seed is easily lost from the pepper-pot seedheads so it is important to keep an eye on them in summer and cut a jarful just as the vents in the top of the pods open and before the wind has a chance to distribute the seed. The hollyhocks at the front of the barn are also redistributed further afield to spread the colony. There must be a vast percentage of seed that perishes, but the seedlings that do find a niche in the gravel are sufficient to give us a display. The random feel of broadcast seed is also more fitting here than that of plants that have been placed, however artfully.

The seed of the best nasturtiums and calendula is also saved as it ripens, so that we do not have to go back to the seed merchants. It is laid out on newspaper for a week to dry so that it is not stored damp and then put into an open jar, and kept in the cool and the dry of the cellar until next spring for re-sowing.

Stringing the onions and harvesting the leaf beet.

The crested cobnuts will be there one day and gone the next, squirrels' eyes being keener than ours. It is a reminder that you need to be vigilant now: ripened summer fruits can easily succumb to competition from wildlife or attacks from fungus once the night dews are again becoming heavier. The autumn-fruiting raspberries need to be regularly harvested under their nets, and the summer-flowering canes removed from the early raspberries so that the new canes can be tied in for next year.

The garlic and onion harvest has been drying in the sun on the terrace. It is important that these do not get wet again before they are plaited for storage. They will be knotted on to a string and brought into the house - one of the most satisfying jobs of the summer. The gourds and squashes are harvested now. They will last for several months on a plate or a shelf but will appreciate a last baking in the sun before they are brought inside.

In dry weather – so that they come out of the ground clean – the last of the potatoes are dug up and stored in paper sacks. They will not produce the poisonous alkaloids that turn them green if they are stored in the dark. The space they leave should have been planted with the winter brassicas, but if they have been left until now, we will sow a last crop of winter salad vegetables under cloches. The tomatoes are grown outside against a south-facing wall so they are late to ripen, which means that they, too, can be susceptible to rot. They are pinched back to three trusses per plant so that the energy is less dispersed, and harvested as soon as they begin to show colour and once the dews have set in. The glut that often occurs at this point means that spare fruit is stored whole in the freezer.

Fresh produce is, of course, always the best but the freezer has revolutionized storage of fruit and vegetables. The gluts that can too easily occur with produce do not have to represent wastage if you have the time to prepare the crop for freezing. Basil and sorrel are made into pesto and the excess beans, raspberries and currants frozen dry in containers. The secret with harvesting is to do it regularly to avoid the produce getting oversized and to encourage cropping. There will always be one courgette that escapes to become a marrow but that seems to be par for the course.

PLANTING BULBS

There is a stillness in the air that is particular to September. Growth has slowed down and is teetering on the edge of decay. The soil is still warm though and, with the potential of moisture once again, it is the perfect time for planting bulbs. The flowering of the colchicums in the gravel at the front is always a good indicator, their naked stems emerging from bare ground are welcome now that the garden is on the gentle slide into autumn.

The beauty of planting bulbs at this point is that they will have a good three months growing time below ground before the soil gets cold and wet. The roots will be able to get a hold before the growing season next year and consequently the bulbs will be well established and more resistant to disease.

It may be hard physically to get into the beds as the growth is still high, so it is a hands and knees job, but you can see the form of the planting still, which makes it easier to plan combinations of summer-flowering bulbs such as allium and galtonia. Remembering the gaps under shrubs and in corners that open up in late winter when the perennials are cut away takes more imagination – a note book helps in these cases to jog the memory.

Bulbs add a swathe of colour early on in the year before most of the perennials have sprung to life and provide interest under the dormant skirts of deciduous shrubs. If they are carefully chosen, bulbs can span a long season. Starting with galanthus in winter, it is easily possible to have something in flower right the way through to the end of summer. They can be used to inject colour and interest amongst summer-flowering perennials, or squeezed into small gaps to enliven associations.

Planting bulbs is best done once you are sure that a planting is settled as they have a tendency to be growing just when you want to move things around. Most bulbs are tolerant

Allium cristophii seedhead.

Seedheads of *Nectaroscordum siculum* subsp. *bulgaricum*.

of being moved when they are growing (in-the-green) and plants like snowdrops actually prefer it, but it is easier to introduce them into an established planting. Having said that, bulbs are wonderfully instant and provide interest early on, which is particularly useful in a young planting.

Choosing varieties that are appropriate to the place is once again important. We have used only small-flowering narcissus for instance, so that the early display has a jewel-like quality. *Narcissus* 'Topolino', a variety that is very similar to our native *N. pseudonarcissus*, though easier to establish, is the first into flower. The native form really needs to be planted in June to establish successfully and even then it can take three years before you get a good show. 'Topolino' is the best early in the garden. It is followed by the pale-flowered 'Dove Wings' and the golden 'Tête-à-Tête' that are used to brighten up dark corners.

Once again, it is important to find the right conditions for the bulbs to thrive. We have had tulips at various points in the garden but they tend to dwindle away after a couple of years so bulbs that naturalize are favoured. The snake's-head fritillary (*Fritillaria meleagris*), has been found a moist spot for instance and the alliums somewhere where they can bake in the sun.

Allium cristophii is used as an injection amongst the perennials on the front terrace. The bulbs like the heat and dryness there and are growing away early before the rosette of leaves is smothered by the perennials around them. They are planted among *Nepeta* 'Six Hills Giant' and through ballota and the bronzed-leaved cow parsley, *Anthriscus* 'Ravenswing'. The later-flowering *Allium sphaerocephalon* is also planted here and it has self-sown freely. It is a fine form with oval dusky-purple flowering heads and grassy foliage that makes a good companion to the red pincushions of knautia in high summer.

Early-flowering bulbs are used to embroider the small circular meadow in the back garden that, at that time of year, is allowed to grow long. The first year one thousand *Crocus tommasinianus* were dug up by the squirrels, every last one of them, so the varieties that we have chosen

Colchicum speciosum with *Verbascum bombyciferum* at the front of the house in late summer. The colchicum needs sunshine and looks best amongst low-growing perennials that will not shade out its winter foliage, which develops soon after the flowers fade. It is best grown in association: the foliage can begin to look tatty as it dies away again in early summer.

subsequently have theft and predators in mind. Over the years, we've discovered that the squirrels seem not to bother with fritillaria, narcissus or *Camassia quamash*.

Bulbs in long grass need a minimum of five weeks after flowering for the leaves to feed the bulbs for the next season, so this little meadow is left until the end of June before it receives its first cut, when it becomes a welcome relief to the burgeoning growth all around – a cool resting place to spill out on.

On the sunny bank at the back *Allium hollandicum* 'Purple Sensation' is used to add spark to the perennials around it. This named variety of the species is a stronger grower, with a more saturated colour that is richer and possibly better. It has self-sown here and some of the young seedlings have reverted to the lavender of the species, but the mix is still pleasant.

Planted in a large drift with break-away clumps to make it feel as if it is a wild colony, it follows on from snowdrops and *Narcissus* 'Dove Wings' which have long since been consumed by the growth of oriental poppies, persicaria and black iris. *Camassia leichtlinii* 'Alba' is used to similar effect amongst the chocolate foliage of the *Artemisia lactiflora* Guizhou Group and *Lysimachia ciliata* 'Firecracker' on the shadier side of the bank.

For the past five years the colony of *Nectaroscordum siculum* in the Lime Enclosure at the front has been added to. They emerge from the ground plane of *Stipa tenuissima* before this planting really gets into motion, teetering on wiry stems. The white satiny bulbs are always a pleasure to handle though they have a tendency to rot if they are not put in soon after they arrive from the supplier. (It is vital that any species bulbs are bought from a reputable source as so many, including our own bluebells, are plundered from the wild.) They will be removed from their paper bags – as all of the bulbs are – and spread out on trays in the barn until they can be planted. Exceptions to this rule are lilies, which are kept just moist in wood shavings until planted.

The general rule is to plant bulbs at about two and a half times their own depth. The ground in the Lime Enclosure is quite free-draining but if it was not, each bulb of the *Nectaroscordum* would be planted on to a small cushion of sharp grit so that water can drain away around them. Grit also protects the bulbs from slugs so with susceptible plants such as lilies, this is standard practice.

Bulbs are always planted in quantity. Every year for four years, one thousand bluebells have been added to the drive to get the sheet of blue that in time will make the entrance sing. It is better to have two breathtaking drifts than variety in tens and twenties. We order a limited number of new bulbs each year from a wholesaler to increase the interest levels in the garden, adding a nought where we can afford it to get the effect that is needed. Of course there are certain treasures such as the erythroniums that are just too expensive to take this approach with. They are best planted when they are growing rather than 'dry' and are bought in as pot-grown plants and nurtured in special corners.

Some plants such as eremurus are not strictly classed as bulbs but will be supplied dry by bulb merchants. September is the moment to plant or divide them. They need to be replanted every five years or so once the clumps become congested. They will have completed their growing cycle by the end of July and withered away so it is important that each crown is marked with a cane. The buds, which are the hub from which the wheel of fleshy roots radiates, are extremely vulnerable in their dormant state, both to the hoe and to footsteps.

Before growth restarts in the autumn the clumps are carefully lifted, as the roots are frighteningly brittle. Congested colonies can easily fall apart once they are out of the ground and the strongest crown should be replanted on a cushion of sharp grit for drainage, with roots spread out in a low depression and then covered with no more than 5cm (2in) of well-drained soil. Grown in the sunniest position available, without competition from anything that can shade their early growth, they will be one of the first plants to start into growth next year, so a winter mulch of bracken or fern leaves is worth the effort in areas prone to heavy frosts.

Planting in quantity demands a degree of patience. If the soil is too dry, which it often is in September, it will be soaked thoroughly the day before so that it is easier to dig into with a trowel. Whether planting into turf or bed space, all bulbs are drifted in informal groups, planting in threes or thirties, depending on size. The look is as soft as it can be when they come through in the spring. From this informal beginning they will start to increase if they are happy and provide the garden with a wave of interest just when it is most needed.

Silver-leaved *Thymus pseudolanuginosus* lining the path in the Thyme Garden.

The Art of Reduction

About ten years ago when only the Woodland Garden had been planted, my father came to see what I was doing. I had valued his comments since we had gardened at home, when I had my yellow border and he a white one, on very separate sides of the same path. A man of few but carefully chosen words, he stood in the garden at Home Farm and said, 'Mmm ... there's a lot going on.' The words sank in deep.

That was the beginning of the reduction process. Despite attempts to garden expansively in what at first appeared to be unlimited space, this was still very much a plantsman's garden. There were miscanthus from the first garden Frances and I had made together in London, macleaya, variegated astrantia, rudbeckia and euphorbias, and there was a whole range of new things that had to be tried and tested. Old-fashioned and species roses, swathes of oriental poppies and iris, and the tree broom (*Genista aetnensis*) because I had never grown it before.

The garden had been planted over three years, moving from the woodland side out east into the sunshine on the bank. Today, the woodland planting remains almost the same as it was when it was planted, but out in the sunshine

A low expanse of *Acaena microphylla* 'Kupferteppich' merges the planting below the limes into the Thyme Garden.

Sanguisorba officinalis 'Tanna', *Sedum telephium* 'Matrona' and *Salvia verticillata* 'Purple Rain' merge into the acaena.

the concept had become blurred and had to be drastically altered for the whole of this area of garden to work together in harmony.

The decision that was arrived at was to treat it as a woodland glade. This involved removing anything that did not feel appropriate to that environment. All the old-fashioned roses were taken away but the species ones retained as they had a more gentle, natural feel. *Rosa rubiginosa* spilled from the woodland and out in the sunshine. *R.* x *odorata* 'Mutabilis' with its single flowers and *R. glauca* were retained as the mood of these plants felt right. The clump of *R. glauca* was added to, spreading the group out across the bank so that its glaucous foliage and autumn hips produced a new anchor for the perennials amongst it.

Anything that was too ornamental was found a new home. The miscanthus were given away because they felt too architectural and formal, and were replaced with a less formal

A large expanse of *Thymus* 'Porlock' is broken by the paler-leaved *T. vulgaris* 'Silver Posie' in the Thyme Garden. The 'Silver Posie' is just coming into flower and will extend the season in this area. Both will be cut back by a third with shears after flowering – a method that keeps the plants from becoming too loose and woody.

grass, *Molinia caerulea* 'Transparent', as its tall veil of flowers and loose growth were more in keeping with the overall look.

In this move towards simplification, one of the first things to go was the variegated astrantia. Today, there is an almost blanket rejection of variegation in the garden; the plants need to feel as close to nature as possible. One of the few exceptions is *Pulmonaria officinalis* 'Sissinghurst White', which has a gentle mottling that is more like dappled light than an obvious ornamentation. The astrantia was replaced with the plain-leaved recurrent flowering subspecies *A. major involucrata* and interplanted with *Lilium martagon*, a combination that I had seen in woodland in the Pyrenees. They were planted in an amorphous drift of two hundred divisions to punch out of the shade of the cornus and into the sun. The drift was picked up with a swathe of *Phlomis russeliana* so that the motion travelled across the whole bank without break. The eye could then flow smoothly from one thing to the next, rather than being distracted by too much choice. The palette was clear, the number of different species replaced with larger quantities of fewer species.

The next project in the Barn Garden took these new principles on board. The meadows beyond, the bright light and the idea of working with hot colour gave us the strong concept and a reduced but homogenous plant palette meant that the planting would have clarity. Certain plants such as *Stipa gigantea* were used in a great arc across the garden and repeats of other plants staggered through the space so that the planting united as a whole. The grasses were limited to no more than three varieties so that their forms would not compete and varieties were chosen that had the same 'feel' about them. This is a rule that has been taken on as a new principle, and an exercise in clarity wherever grasses are used.

The planting has become increasingly confident with each new area cultivated. Simple forms have dominated, with reduced and homogenous collections of plants selected to provide as much interest for as long as possible. The gems are woven in as surprises so that you can find them on closer observation. That way they are less demanding of your attention and you can feel the mood first before discovering the hidden treasure.

Moving out from the simplicity of the Lime Enclosure, three large mounds of yew were planted to draw on the forms of the trees and distant hills in the background. It was clear that the view from the front terrace to the area that the pond now occupies would need to be plain. The eye should be encouraged out to a broader view. We tried a small meadow initially, which very soon confused the picture as it was altogether too small. It was removed in less than a season and replaced with the thyme planting, which you can look out, and over, from the terrace rather than look in to.

Wrapping around the Lime Enclosure, the planting could afford to be more complex as it had to connect with the Barn Garden. There the framed view of the barn doors demanded a composition that worked from either direction.

The planting below the limes uses the mood of the landscape beyond. There are grasses, ornamental yarrows and burnets. *Molinia caerulea* 'Windspiel' has been leapfrogged into

The planting below the limes is low and expansive. It anchors the lower section of the barn and frames the view through into the Barn Garden beyond when the barn doors are open.

the Lime Enclosure here. Planted in front of the barn doors, it emerges through an expansive drift of *Salvia verticillata* 'Purple Rain'. Fifty plants were used to create the drift. At its height in summer the salvia casts a dusky swathe across this piece of the garden that registers from afar. You can see it through the lime trunks back on the drive. It has a landscape feel about it – the simplicity of distant fields.

Close to the barn, the terracotta-flowered *Achillea* 'Walther Funcke' makes the link with the orange of the ironstone and the colour inside the Barn Garden. Achilleas need just the right free-draining spot to remain intact as perennials. Winter wet and the slugs in spring are their worst enemies when the growth is young.

Emerging from the salvia early on is the giant fennel (*Ferula communis*), which, when planted as a young seedling, is able to put its roots down deep, to flower after a couple of years of building up strength. The seeds of the fennel are saved and sown immediately as they have a short viability. Some are sown directly into a gap in the planting so that they will not need to be disturbed and their long tap roots can establish themselves, while others are sown into long toms and planted out when their roots reach the bottom. These are used to replace the older plants, which die in the process of flowering.

The forms of later-flowering plants assert themselves over the season: thimble-flowered *Sanguisorba officinalis* 'Tanna', and the sculptural *Sedum telephium* 'Matrona'. This sedum is a hefty grower and one plant can cartwheel out to 1m (3ft) across by the autumn. Although I have never tried it, sedum can be discouraged from doing this by being lifted with a spade in the spring – not moved, but just disturbed so that the energy goes back into the roots and the fleshy top-growth is curtailed. There is enough space in this planting, so they are allowed to have their own character and are left alone. Late in autumn the salvia and sedum are broken by the mound-forming *Aster lateriflorus* 'Horizontalis', which moves down to a vast swathe of *Acaena microphylla* 'Kupferteppich'. The aster has been copper too for most of the summer. Its leaves are one of its best assets, but it is also worth growing for its resistance to mildew.

In front of the house the planting is further reduced. The thyme lawn has no more than a line of desire scored into it like a little animal track and three different thymes that come into flower in succession and change like moving cloud shadows on the ground. *Thymus* 'Porlock' is in flower first, its dark green foliage giving way to a mass of lilac flower early in the summer. Then 'Silver Posie' takes over and finally *T. pseudolanuginosus* follows on. The display lasts for two months and then the planting reverts to greens.

Achillea 'Walther Funcke' adds bite to the expanse of *Salvia verticillata* 'Purple Rain' outside the barn doors. This is a reliable drought-resistant variety of achillea but it needs a free-draining site to avoid it rotting in the winter months. Behind it is the pale-flowered *Santolina pinnata* subsp. *neapolitana* 'Edward Bowles', becoming more informal now that it is growing out after its spring pruning. Until it flowers, its tight growth adds a sculptural mounding to this soft informal planting.

10

OCTOBER

LIGHT

The forgiving light of autumn has softened as the angle of the sun tilts away. It is almost a relief after the harsh overhead glare of summer, which can flatten the garden for most of the day and bleach colour to such an extent that it is almost invisible. Summer is the time to garden early or late in the day to get the benefit of indirect light, or to seek out shadows in the middle of the day.

Rosa virginiana.

Stipa gigantea has been in flower now in the Barn Garden since late May, catching the early morning light in its inflorescences. It is joined in autumn by the shorter and tighter-growing *Molinia caerulea* subsp. *arundinacea* 'Moorhexe'. Of the two, molinia prefers a damper position but is happy once it is established, as the soil is heavy and rich in the Barn Garden.

Now, though, the soft light of autumn brings out the warmth of the garden again. It will rake and pull at shadows and illuminate spent summer growth, colouring berries and leaves, teasing out the best things in this season.

One of the most mood-altering elements, light is often neglected in a garden. It is all too easy to look at light in crude terms of sun and shade, but there is dappled shade with its depth and its sparkling intensity, and there are all the nuances that can happen over the course of a day, a week or a season.

The light at Home Farm very much dictates the way in which the garden is used. The Woodland Garden at the back of the house is most interesting at the beginning and the end of the day. In the morning, the garden will be side-lit from the east so the pale light-catching spires of the *Persicaria amplexicaulis* 'Rosea' are illuminated. In the late afternoon

Cirsium rivulare
'Atropurpureum' (top).
Molinia caerulea
'Transparent' (centre).
Populus alba (below).

and the evening the sun will shaft through the trees of the adjoining wood, casting a dappled shade and back-lighting the cirsium and ruby-red of *Cotinus coggygria* 'Royal Purple'. The cotinus has been carefully placed so that its leaves can be back-lit in the afternoon. They are as good as stained glass at this moment and without the benefit of back-lighting, half the magic of this plant would be lost.

Mid-day is the worst time to be in this garden as the sun has not yet swung around into the trees. The colours flatten in the glare of overhead light and it is difficult to define form so we have had to interplant this south-facing bank with tall woody material to cast shadows and maintain the mystery here. The bushes of *Rosa* x *odorata* 'Mutabilis' are now so tall that they cast shadows on to the little lawn beside them – one good reason for the smooth surface of cut grass in summer. The sorbus add depth to the garden by pooling shade around the perimeter. The depth that shadows bring to the garden is essential as they add weight and volume. They are the dark accent that brightness needs as contrast and, in the shade, plants will be allowed to glow and sparkle. The dew on the alchemilla will be all the brighter and blues will glow with an intensity that would be lost in the sunshine.

Seating is carefully placed to take advantage of the light. Over the years we have taken time to see exactly where it falls and how it moves across the garden in a day. The yew shelter comes into its own in the middle of the day, a dark cave from which the garden can be observed. The shelter faces south-west to take advantage of the afternoon light, which will back-light everything from this point. In the Barn Garden we have two seats: a bench against the wall, facing east to view the garden in the morning, and two stone plinths at ground level on the other side, to see the garden with the sun behind it later on in the day.

The light-absorbing flowering heads of the grasses are perhaps one of the most effective ways of harnessing the light in the garden. Their open plumage allows the light

Late afternoon light illuminating the ironstone of the
barn wall.

to penetrate the forms, where it is caught on each filament. In the Barn Garden, *Stipa gigantea*
will become incandescent in the early morning – the light is literally caught in the tall
inflorescences. But to benefit from this illumination, they have to be grown in the open
or at least in a position that sets them between you and the sun. The Lime Enclosure at
the front of the house is positioned between the light source and the observation point so
that it is back-lit for most of the day and then side-lit in the afternoon. Sea lavender (*Limonium
platyphyllum*) is another plant with an open cage of growth that benefits from this orientation.
It will glow lavender in summer and then a hot cinnamon as the flowers fade.

The trunks of the limes catch low light that would otherwise be lost if it were not intercepted.

The solid objects in the garden are just as important as those with filamentous growth or translucent foliage. Cut topiary forms are used in very much the same way to harness the low rays of the sun. In the winter they are at their best with long shadows cast for many times their own height across the ground, charting the movement of the sun as long as it is shining. The west-facing barn wall is a spectacle in the evening light as it will flood the garden with a wall of colour. Out in the landscape, the velvet green corrugations of the ridge-and-furrow fields to the east catch the low rays of the rising sun for a short but wonderful interlude at dawn and then lose their definition as the sun rises. There is a real magic in this transition. The hills behind them will be dark then: as the sun rises over them, depending upon the time of year, they will turn brown or emerald or golden or blond.

THE LAST FLING

The first frosts and shortening days bring with them a shift of mood; the tension of expectation has gone as the garden breathes out and falls into repose. The four seasons are marked by such dramatic changes in the landscape that it is impossible not to be affected and to see the world again with a different take. You have to relax into autumn to really enjoy the informality of it. There is a wonder in the shift into the next season.

There is no point in fighting the decay or the disorder as the plants let go and begin to recede. The leaves that fall to the ground will rapidly decay or be pulled into the soil by earthworms to replenish the goodness that has been removed over the summer. Leaves will need to be cleared only where they drift deep and smother small plants or where they congest lawns or silver plants that need plenty of air around them. To maintain a sense

The ridge-and-furrow fields revealed not long after dawn. As the sun rises, their corrugations appear to flatten.

of order all we do at this point is to keep the paths raked so that there is a contrast. It is a simple device but one that keeps the garden from feeling entirely neglected.

The change in the garden starts quite early on with the colouring up of the *Aralia elata* behind the house as it flecks with scarlet and burgundy in August. At that point the garden still has quite a way to go until autumn, but the change here is always worth it. On a good still year, the long pinnate leaves of the aralia will be a spectacle for two weeks, but if we are lucky and the wind whips around the corner of the house, they will be blown to tatters and the stems left naked while the rest of the garden is still in full leaf. They are worth the effort they take, but having grown them here I would never again put them in such an exposed position.

Nearby, in the shade of the house, there is a group of the Virginian pokeweed (*Phytolacca americana*) that, late in the summer, rises up from its fleshy rootstock to waist height. Over the spring it will form a modest but handsome pile of oval leaves that give way to white pokers of flower. From late summer onwards the pokers develop their evil-looking black berries that carry through to the frosts, at which point the whole plant will be felled to the ground. In the wrong situation it could easily become a weed so it is kept contained here in the gravel, where its numerous seedlings are easily hoed out. Although this plant gives some people the horrors – and rightly so because its berries are extremely toxic – it has an exotic, sinister appeal that seems appropriate here in the shade.

The last spires of the *Persicaria amplexicaulis* 'Alba' are very necessary in the Woodland Garden as they give it an extra lift when it might otherwise look tired. *Cimicifuga simplex* var. *simplex* 'Brunette' will pick up the vertical accents with its own tapering flower spikes. This is an elegant plant, if you can grow it. Slow to establish, it needs a cool atmosphere, a little shade and a moist root-run for its foliage not to burn. The dusky purple leaves are perhaps one of its greatest attributes, so it is worth making an effort to find it the right position. *Geranium procurrens* is another plant that will enliven this shade planting. From late summer onwards, it will throw out sparse but vibrant flowers that are an intense violet with a dark magenta eye. The colour resonates in shade and is wonderful with the rich greens of the ferns and wood-sedge here. It has to be controlled at points over the summer as it is a great colonizer, running in agile streamers over the heads of other groundcover. It wastes no time and where it touches down it will root. In autumn, occasional leaves will begin to colour scarlet and crimson, a tendency which is also particular to the semi-evergreen *G. macrorrhizum*. These flecks of colour are a bonus.

The ripening burrs of *Acaena microphylla* 'Kupferteppich' will turn this evergreen mat-forming perennial from ruby red to rust over the autumn months.

Hips on *Rosa virginiana*. This single-flowered dog-rose is slightly later flowering than the other 'wild' roses. Forming a shrub 2m (6½ft) high and as much across, the growth is almost thornless. It is wind, drought and pest resistant.

The berrying plants are one of the great joys of this season and some of the best are the native plants used to integrate the garden into the surrounding countryside. The scarlet berries of the mountain ash are spectacular early on but are first to succumb to feeding birds. The indigo fruits on the blackthorn hang on until the leaves are down, as do those of sweetbriars. The straight species of our guelder rose (*Viburnum opulus*) is used in groups in the screen planting along the drive with *Cornus sanguinea,* which is now colouring crimson. The viburnum is hung with blood-red berries that will persist in a mild winter until they are either withered by weather or eaten by birds. In the Woodland Garden the amber-berried selection of this plant, *V. opulus* 'Xanthocarpum' is used to merge the wood with the garden. Now it is hung with translucent fruit that ripen from bitter yellow to amber.

The roses, too, come into their own again with a crop of hips. *Rosa glauca* is one of the best, with dark mahogany fruits but they are so good that they are stripped by the birds as soon as they are ripe, a great fluttering of activity letting you know that it is feeding time. Others tend to hold on to their hips for longer. On the edge of the Woodland Garden there is a large clump of *Rosa virginiana*, which has never presented us with any problems over the twelve years that it has been there. Gently suckering, it flowers slightly later than the other dog-roses but continues to provide interest with fine glossy leaves that colour vividly. Now, hung with a heavy crop of small rounded hips, it is one of the most glorious plants in this part of the garden. The hips will hang heavy on the dark branches until the weather is hard in the winter. They are obviously not the delicacy that *R. glauca* is but they will be eaten eventually.

In the Barn Garden, the bleached out grasses are infused with flecks of ruby-red from the large pendulous hips of the *Rosa* 'Scharlachglut'. The shrubs are arching over at about 2m (6ft) now that they are established and they balance the *Rosa moyesii* on the far side of the garden. There are two varieties of this vivid dog-rose in the garden. I bought five plants from two different sources. The two strongest are

Molinia caerulea subsp. *arundinacea* 'Windspiel' just at the point when they turn from straw to apricot to butter-yellow. They will hold together this planting in the Lime Enclosure late into autumn.

the straight species with vermilion flowers. They are now more than 2.5m (8ft) and hung with dark orange flagon-shaped hips. The less vigorous of the two is the variety 'Geranium', which is bright crimson and more compact in habit.

Autumn colour works best on a grand scale and now that the pond is in place, the generous planting at the front has begun to take on a 'landscape' feel. *Molinia caerulea* 'Windspiel' has a brief but wonderful moment of glory before being driven over by the wind, when it colours butter-yellow – exactly the same luminous colouring as the larch in Tom's Wood. *Acaena microphylla* 'Kupferteppich' at their feet turns an extraordinary burnt red as the seed heads ripen. The willows fleck, their tiny leaves colouring pale yellow before they drop to cast a luminous shadow underneath them that marks the end of one season and the beginning of the next.

PLANTING AND PROPAGATION

A window of opportunity appears in autumn that allows us to take stock. The garden is tall but growth is mostly spent and we can afford the time now to relax and let the autumn take over. The soil, however, is still warm, and where possible, the first of the autumn planting can begin. Although the planting season continues until April whenever the weather permits, autumn and early winter are still the best times to plant deciduous plants. They then have a chance to get a hold in their new home before the onset of winter and by spring they will grow away fast. Although it may not look as if much is happening above ground, roots will continue to grow in all but the coldest of periods when the ground is frost-laden.

For this reason we try to get all deciduous trees and shrubs in by Christmas. Although they can be planted right up until bud-burst, they will then be delayed in growth and will need more water in the first year, their roots not having gained a grip before the top growth begins. Evergreens, however, are best planted or moved in late winter, particularly species such as lavender and santolina, which can perish in the wet and cold of winter. They will often die of drought because their leaves are still loosing water but their roots are unable to extract it from the ground because the water is frozen. These plants are best kept moist in the shelter of a cold frame until planting time. Plants held in containers of any kind over the winter are at their most vulnerable if they become waterlogged. The combination of wet and cold can be lethal, so although it would be wrong not to water, it is best to err on the side of caution.

Knowing your plants or, at least, having a good idea about what they like and dislike, ensures that every plant can be given an environment in which it will thrive, with a suitable aspect and appropriate soil. A penny spent on the plant and a pound on the hole is an important point to remember, in order to give them a good start in life. That means taking time to understand the soil, to see that it drains well but retains moisture and making sure that it is improved enough with compost or manure for the plant to make a smooth transition to its new environment. Follow-on care in the first season is also important. New introductions will often need extra watering and a careful eye cast over them to ensure that they are free from competition, pests and diseases. Competition between neighbouring plants or weeds will rob the soil of water and essential minerals.

The range of plant material that has been used to stock the garden has, on the whole, been small and young. We have been prepared to wait for plants to mature and would rather spend money on larger numbers of small plants than larger and fewer plants for what might appear to be immediate effect. Young plants are like children: they will adapt faster to a new environment. Whether they are container-grown or bare-root specimens, they tend to establish faster and will outstrip larger plants, which take longer to adjust to new soil and a new climate, and will need additional staking and watering.

Over the years trees have been planted extensively on the property, but again we have used young plants in the main, to keep costs down. Young two-year-old plants (known as whips) have been used to plant our woodland and hedges. Tom's Wood was slit-planted as whips twelve years ago and is now already towering above us. Slit-planting is easy and fast and is reserved for native plants that will integrate themselves rapidly into their new home. It simply involves inserting a spade to make a narrow slit and slipping the roots of the young plant into it. A heel pressed firmly at the base of the plant will close the slit up

Most of the trees at Home Farm have been planted as small whips and feathered maidens, seen here heeled into the stock bed. Feathered maidens have been favoured over larger standards because they still have their lower branches, which gives the plants a softer, more natural look. They are less dependent on staking (although they will need to be secured in the first season to a cane or a short stake in a windy situation) and establish faster, outstripping a larger tree in two to three years.

Sarah (centre and right) planting some young standard fruit trees below the barn. On the few occasions that standards are used, a stake is knocked into the hole on the windward side of the tree so that the stem will blow away from the stake and be less prone to rubbing. Trees should always be replanted at the same depth that they were growing at – a cane placed across the hole will give you a height to match the rootball to, before refilling the hole. The stake should only measure about a third of the height of the stem. Anchored low, the stem will then flex and strengthen along its length, forming a stronger trunk. The tree should be fastened securely, but not tightly, with a rubber tie and the soil firmed in around the roots to remove air pockets. Rabbit guards may be necessary in some areas.

again. The secret here is to keep the roots of the young plants moist. Left for even a few minutes in a cold wind, they will dry and damage, so keep them in a moistened bag until the last minute when planting.

Ornamental shrubs, climbers and larger grown trees are all given a good start, which involves thorough preparation. A hole that is a third as big again as the root ball, both in terms of depth and width, is the minimum requirement. Whether planting as bare-root or containerized plants, a good half-spit of manure or compost is worked into the base of the hole and a couple of spades full into the topsoil, along with a handful of bonemeal. Plants need loose soil around their roots so that the fibrous and fine roots can move freely.

A new plant should always be planted at the same depth at which it was growing in the nursery. With bare-root plants, there will be a soil mark on the stem to indicate this.

Containerized plants should also be thoroughly wetted before being planted, by plunging them in a bucket of water until the bubbles stop surfacing. Watering them in afterwards, particularly in spring, so that the soil makes contact with the roots, gives them the best chance to bond with their new environment.

When planting perennials, soil preparation will take place over the whole area rather than for each individual plant. This involves forking a barrow load of well-rotted compost or manure per square metre into the top spit to give the young plants the head start they need. We tend to plant in large drifts in the garden to mimic the way nature disperses plants over a piece of ground. Larger mother colonies will form the mass while break-away satellites (anything from five to one lone plant), will give the impression that they have sown themselves away from the original group. This method of planting adds fluidity to the garden.

People have often wondered at the sheer numbers of plants we use to achieve this fluidity. Planting in tens, and multiples of ten, has become second nature here. It has meant that we have often had to be patient and propagate plants ourselves to economize on resources. The *Alchemilla mollis* plants were a good example. The first year saw us preparing the site that they were to be planted into. In tandem, five large plants were bought in and each divided into five in the autumn, each piece having a good growing tip and strong roots. The twenty-five divisions were planted into a small nursery area and the following autumn divided up again into the 125 plants we needed to drift through the gravel at the rear of the house. All the astrantias and many of the more vigorous perennials were treated in this way. The grasses are always divided in the spring once they have started to grow. (It is easy to kill grasses if they are moved at the wrong end of the season.) They are cut into four sections with a serrated knife so that each quarter has a good amount of root to sustain it.

Not all the propagation is as straightforward. The knautias and *Digitalis ferruginea* are bulked up and replaced each year by potting up self-sown seedlings and growing them on in a cold frame. The eldest plants last only two to three years, so an on-going programme of replacement is essential to keep the numbers up.

Cuttings are kept to a minimum as they require constant maintenance, but we do take heel cuttings of purple sage (*Salvia officinalis* Purpurascens Group), santolina and lavender each July to replace plants that have dwindled. They are plunged into a friable mix in the cold frames and potted up in September, held in the frames and planted out in the spring. Hardwood cuttings of willows, cornus and buddleia are taken as soon as the leaves have fallen, a pencil-thick section 30cm (12in) long being enough to set roots over the winter and spring. The effects may not be immediate but propagating your own is worth the wait.

Autumn is an ideal time to split perennials – the soil is still warm and there is time for the roots to re-establish.

NOVEMBER

11

TEXTURE

As the profusion of the past six months ebbs away and the cloak of colour and vegetation recedes again, the landscape of the garden is revealed in a new light. The underlying skeletons begin to poke through, the stark burst of growth on the limes is bared against the sky, with a burst of red shoots that gives warmth in the grey days. The dark weight of the yew mounds seems to grow in stature as the foliage around them ebbs away. Sepia, greys and browns replace the greens and the hot autumn colours.

The limes once the leaves are down.

With wood ripened for the winter ahead and next year's buds tight and safe, the garden at Home Farm begins its hibernation.

This season, however, is far from desolate: it is simply a case of retraining the eye. Stripped back now that the distraction of summer is gone, the garden reveals a rich patina of textures and forms. You are aware of the surfaces in the garden, low light picking out the rounded, time-worn undulations in the cobbles and the fissures in the slabs on the terrace that were upturned to reveal their rough surfaces. The plants, too, seem to offer up another layer of interest, the thyme lawn with its tight mossiness is dense and matt like a velvet pile and the close-knit texture of the yew foliage allows us to read its curves.

One of the most interesting shifts at this time of year is the way in which the evergreens take on an altogether new role. The *Magnolia grandiflora* on the terrace was opulence personified during the summer with its bowls of scented flower, but now its foliage is the focus. This variety, 'Exmouth', has much the best foliage of those available and the form is open and not stunted. The placing of this tree gave us many hours of debate over the years. It is highly ornamental and rather grand with it, but as it developed its own character, it began to settle in to the warm corner of the buildings, the rust undersides of its leaves matching the colour of the stone. The texture of the undersides is one of the joys of this plant; being absolutely matt, like suede, they are a complete contrast to the polished surfaces of the upper sides. These are brilliant and reflective on a sunny day, as if the whole tree is hung with mirrors that shimmer and refract light.

Altogether more appropriate to Home Farm, the hollies perform in much the same way in the winter, glinting and reflecting light on a bright day. It is odd how they go unnoticed in the summer, but winter is their true season. There is one ancient tree on the boundary that gives the Woodland Garden depth and gravity. It inspired a whole new planting at the back of the garden, using the darkness of holly in groups to sink and blur the edges, while the lightness of the deciduous *Sorbus aria* 'Lutescens' adds sparkle in the summer months.

Young pot-grown hollies were planted amongst a group of five sorbus in this area but twelve years on there is a discrepancy between the two. The silver sorbus are several metres high and in the prime of their youth, but the tallest of the hollies is just 2m (6ft) tall. Like all slow burners, they will make their presence felt eventually. The hollies are desperately slow and hate competition from anything else so we have had to be patient and keep them free of close neighbours, resisting the temptation to add any shrubs to fill the gap.

It has been important that the 'feel' of the Woodland Garden has a softness to it. Woodlands are places that give under foot – mosses, ferns and fallen leaves creating a mood that is gentle and tactile. Now that the little path has been cut into Tom's Wood, we can experience the rich diversity of textures in the woodland there. Cracked and fissured pine trunks,

Magnolia grandiflora 'Exmouth'.

Spent heads on the *Phlomis russeliana*. The leaves of this
plant are evergreen and form an impenetrable groundcover,
so much so that they have to be placed alongside other
plants that can hold their own – such as bronze fennel,
bronze sage and *Euphorbia characias*. This combination will go
on to maintain textural interest for the whole of the winter.

satiny prunus and corky field maple are all irresistible to the touch. On the woodland floor
the mossy growth of the cow parsley and the puckered leaves of the primroses all add to
the experience of being there.

Texture has played an important part in the way in which the Woodland Garden at
the back of the house has developed. The brick paths have been laid and pointed with
sand so that mosses are encouraged to colonize them and the planting is gentle. At ground
level, the hart's-tongue ferns will pick up the light on their polished evergreen leaves and
so will *Helleborus foetidus* when the foliage is wet. But it is important to have contrast to make
the shine brighter: like the positive and negative of the magnolia leaves, plants with shiny
leaves need juxtaposing with those that are absolutely matt. The ferns, for instance, are
interplanted through the felty matt *Geranium macrorrhizum* for contrast. We also play with
scale in texture here, using small, undemanding foliage such as that of *Galium odoratum*
and tiarella to create a groundcovering eiderdown from which the plants with a stronger
texture can emerge.

Stipa tenuissima, a true grass, in the background with *Carex testacea*, a sedge.

The silvered leaves of the biennial *Verbascum bombyciferum* form a vast evergreen rosette.

Melianthus major in a sheltered corner with self-sown *Eryngium giganteum*.

The trunks in the beech copse, one of the original features at Home Farm.

At the front of the property, texture has played a different role. Here we needed to establish a link with the pastoral landscape beyond. The close-knit undemanding texture of the yews allows them to register as form and the fine tussocky grasses make the link with the meadow land beyond. The diversity of textures has been reduced here to ones that the eye can pass over, so they are mostly fine and matt. It is only when you look into the planting that the detail becomes apparent. The felty mulleins and the spiky eryngiums provide a subtle contrast to the wiry grasses, and the filigree-like rue adds blue pillows of softness that remain in place for the winter. The more you look at this time of year, the more you see.

The layering of the fields is made part of the garden by replacing the hedgeline with a fence on the boundary. Similarly, the planting below the Barn Garden (previous pages) is linked both to the buildings and the countryside beyond. It flows from the garden and forms a bond between the enclosed and the open. Its low informality allows the eye to pass out into the landscape beyond.

Deciduous hawthorns open up the view in the winter. Hawthorns are higly valued at Home Farm as they are one of the richest host trees for wildlife in this country.

BOUNDARIES

Creating an ornamental garden in a pastoral setting has been one of the great challenges at Home Farm and most of the 'gardened' spaces have had to be given their own boundaries for them not to jar with the landscape beyond. These enclosures have become safe places in which to gain confidence and develop moods that are particular to each place.

Despite the need to work within these self-imposed confines, there were always references to the landscape so that the 'gardened' garden felt as integrated as possible. We used native plants or varieties of them to smudge the end of one environment and the start of the next. The adjoining woodland was encouraged to 'spill' into the garden at the back with plants that felt as if they had moved from the wood itself into the garden. The hedges were replanted with indigenous hedging plants: hawthorn (*Crataegus monogyna*), blackthorn (*Prunus spinosa*), guelder rose (*Viburnum opulus*), hazel (*Corylus avellana*) and dog-rose (*Rosa canina*), and the fences and gates were in keeping with those found in the farmland around us. Within the ornamental planting, yew and box forms were shaped to refer to the trees and hills in the landscape beyond, so that the eye leapt naturally from one to the next without actually having to travel the real distance.

Views were maintained out of the enclosures to retain the link. The canopies of the limes were raised up on stilts so that you could see beyond the Grass Garden by looking between the trunks. Once the hedge was grown around the Barn Garden, it was cut into a gentle undulation so that it felt as if it was part of the hills in the distance. These were all simple devices but they worked.

Over the years, however, our confidence grew and with it the commitment to forge a way out into the land beyond the inner gardens, so that the narrative of the garden could really encompass the surrounding landscape. We wanted to be able to stroll and meander through the different environments, to interact with the calm of simple shade and to turn our backs on the 'gardened' garden to embrace the real countryside.

The development of the pond took twelve years of discussion but it was the solution that was needed to pull the garden together finally. As soon as the excavation for the pond filled with water, the garden was changed completely. Your eye no longer rested upon the planting at the front, but passed over it to the reflective qualities of the water. Despite the fact that we had been nervous about changing the landscape of the field, we were amazed at the impact this action made upon the feeling of space and how it encouraged the desire to go out into the land to experience its difference.

The knock-on effect of creating the pond made us want to explore this new territory, so a route was forged out into the land to make a circuit that would pick up on the paths that had, until then, taken a more intimate route through the gardens adjoining the buildings. The new path would explore the whole area and work on the eighteenth-century landscape principle of exploring the very boundaries of the property, thus enhancing the feeling of space. The walk would link us with the pasture that borders the property and give us a reason for travelling out into the grounds. It would give the garden a new perspective.

We started in winter, while the pond excavations lay heavy and wet, by cutting a way into Tom's Wood. This was an area that had been planted as a native copse twelve years ago in an 'L' section of the field that lay on the western side of the property. The copse was designed to screen the land from the village and to filter the prevailing wind that cut from the south-west. Back then, establishing a little wood seemed like a long-term plan and we left the trees to develop, doing little more than keeping them free of competition in the early years. But the developments pushed us to venture into this area again and in that time the young saplings had grown to 6–9m (20–30ft). They had formed a new environment that could be embraced as part of the garden.

Cutting a way into the trees took not much more than a day, and we chose a route that would lead from the pond side and take us as close to the boundary as possible without being aware of the perimeter. We planted bluebells and snowdrops in-the-green to line the path and divided some primroses from the garden at the back of the house. Some reclaimed posts and a piece of oak planking formed a small seat as a stopping-off point on the way and, when the spring came, we mowed a path into the cow parsley that had colonized the new shade there to mark the way.

As soon as the excavated land from the pond was dry enough, it was re-contoured so that it flowed on into the landscape and a little depression was cut around the back of the pond, to mark what would feel like a well-trodden way that would guide us on the new circuit. Once the newly sown meadow grew, a path was cut into it along the depression to flow on from the little meadow at the back of the barn. The route now split beside the barn. You could take one inner route to view the 'gardened' garden, moving into the Barn Garden to do so, and another to view and interact with the landscape.

This simple move trebled the feeling of space in the garden as the walk took us to the very edges of the property. We could now get close to the animals in the pasture and

Steve and I constructing a small 'interlude' along the track in Tom's Wood. This bench is made from nothing more than recycled materials found on the property – an old telegraph pole, an oak plank and some nails.

glimpse acres of land that seemed as if they were part of the garden. The eye could travel. The new circuit cut through the small meadow to the rear of the barn to view the ridge-and-furrow fields to the east and then moved into the silver wood, where the contrasting cut grass caught the shadows of the white poplars. From there you gained your first view of the water, looking along its length to the young saplings of Tom's Wood in the distance. The garden felt as if it was part of the landscape again. It was a new feeling that was both calming and expansive.

Swinging round behind the pond, the path switched between the old trees on the boundary that we had never visited before and turned back towards the house at the jetty, where a reflected image of the house revealed itself in the water. Turning your back on the house again, the path moved on from the lightness there and plunged into the shade of Tom's Wood, through the cow parsley and the hazel coppice before emerging again at the beginning of the drive – a meander of half an hour or so. The narrative was complete.

Hazel twigs are used to form plant supports soon after they have been harvested and whilst they are still supple. Pushed into the ground, the tops are bent over and secured with string to form a cage, which plants can grow up through over the summer.

COPPICE

When we planted the native copse that has now become Tom's Wood, a quarter of the land towards the drive was planted with *Corylus avellana*, the indigenous hazel. The little whips took what seemed to be a painful amount of time to establish, despite the fact that they were kept clear of competition in the first three years. Hazel are woodlanders by nature and hated the open grassland that they had been introduced to. After five years they were interplanted with some young willow cuttings that quickly grew up to produce the cool shade they craved and, ten years after planting, the first hazel were ready to coppice.

I visited an old site on the South Downs to learn how this was done. The woodsmen had set up camp amongst the coppice and were living on the land during the harvesting period. The trees were felled to the base with a sharp hand-axe and the wood graded for making hurdles and stakes, and for brushwood for pea sticks. The hurdles were being made on site in much the same way as they had been for a thousand years.

I learnt that the best time to coppice was in the first part of the winter, as soon as the leaves had fallen, when the sap was low and the wood at its most pliable. Harvested once the sap has risen, the trees would have less reserves to regenerate strong and straight, and the wood would last less well once it was cut.

A managed coppice has a magic all of its own. The oldest coppices in this country are more than a thousand years old and they get better and richer with age, the stumps of the old hazel growing ever more gnarled and fantastic, the woodland floor more diverse. Cut to the ground on an eight- to ten-year cycle, a coppice is constantly in flux, always regenerating and changing. The shaded woodland floor will erupt with life that has been dormant once the wood is cut away at the end of this cycle. When cleared of their stems so that the trees are reduced to little more than stumps, the sun will penetrate the earth, activating new life that has been dormant for a decade. Instead of trees, foxgloves and bluebells, violets, primroses and wood

The hazel is coppiced soon after the leaves have fallen in the autumn, cut as low as possible with a sharp blade. New shoots will form in the spring. These will be able to be harvested again in eight to ten years time.

anemones will reign for three years or so before the canopy closes over and the wait resumes until the land is once again harvested.

The whole concept of regeneration is all the more exciting when the product from the cycle can be used in the garden. Stakes, pea sticks and flexible branches to weave into plant supports would all be needed on an annual basis. With 30 trees in the coppice, our plan was to cut three trees a year, so that by the time the last was cut, the first would once again be ready.

The hazels are not the only plants that are coppiced in the garden, though they are the only ones that provide a usable product. Coppicing elsewhere is used as a technique to promote strong growth, or growth that is more colourful and eye-catching. Over the years we have developed a technique of partial coppicing in some plants and complete coppicing in others, bending the horticultural rules a little to get the effect that is needed in the garden.

Rubus thibetanus is cut every year at the end of the winter when the new growth is emerging at the base of the plant so that the whole shrub can regenerate from ground level. The new stems are dusted with a white down. Left unpruned, the old stems would taint the effect as their brightness dims over the year. After such drastic treatment, the plants are always mulched with a collar of manure and given a handful of blood, fish and bone so that they have the energy do it again. This is vital treatment: the plants will rapidly dwindle without it. They need feeding to perform well.

Although the books recommend it, we do not cut either of the cornus to the base to promote their coloured stems. In the soft informality of the Woodland Garden, they would feel too ornamental. The red tips on the *Cornus alba* 'Aurea' are enough to light up the garden in winter and the black stems of 'Kesselringii' are all the better for being treated with a little less severity, as this is a less strongly growing variety. Instead of reducing all the growth to the ground every second or third year, a third of the oldest growth is removed annually to the base so that there is always height in the plant and always a fresh crop of new stems to keep the plants from getting too woody and losing their colour. The feeding remains an integral part of the process.

The new willows around the pond will be coppiced to the ground every third year to promote strongly coloured stems. We have two varieties of *Salix daphnoides* around the water, 'Aglaia' which is a dark mahogany and 'Oxford Violet' which is dusted with a mauve bloom. The thunder-sky colour of these stems is needed here in great drifts in the winter. The darkness will ground the vegetation and link it with the muted colours of the field and wooded hill in the background. Behind the barn we also have *Salix irrorata*, whose pale whitened stems are the same colour as the lichens on the walls. These are pruned also on a three-year cycle, but the pruning cuts are made at knee-height so that the plant will develop a gnarled character appropriate to the age of the barn.

Coppicing is not only employed as a means of promoting coloured stems. The biennial canes of the summer raspberries are cut to the base after they have fruited to make way

Salix irrorata is coppiced every two to three years to produce strong, brightly coloured stems for the winter. These stems are not used for staking as they root so easily that the garden would soon be full of willow.

for new growth and the autumn-fruiting raspberries coppiced to the ground at the beginning of winter, as they fruit on the current year's growth and not the previous. *Rosa glauca* is razed to the ground every four or five years in mid-winter and given a good feed so it will regrow strongly. It seems a drastic thing to do but the new foliage produced is bluer and lusher for it and the stems a richer shade of violet in the winter. This technique can be carried out on a shorter three-year cycle, but ours suits the garden.

Back out in the woodland, selective trees are coppiced to promote multi-stemmed growth so that not all the trees rise from a single trunk. Not everything will appreciate such drastic treatment but it adds to the variation that makes the copse special. We pruned some of the bird cherries (*Prunus padus*), the alders (*Alnus cordata*) and the hornbeam (*Carpinus betulus*) back hard to the ground after the three years to encourage new shoots to regrow. They were then left to themselves to develop in their own way, the idiosyncratic nature of the regrowth adding to the experience of the woodland.

12 DECEMBER

MATERIALS

The old stone walls at Home Farm are one of its best features. We have gone to great lengths during the garden's development to find materials that would blend and recede into the overall picture. Nothing should shout out that it was a new introduction.

White berries of black-stemmed *Cornus alba* 'Kesselringii'.

Although the new landscaping underpins the planting, giving us the direction, the hardstanding and a means of moving about in the garden, it has never been meant to read as a great statement. Sourcing local materials is half the battle, as they blend with the walls and soil, and immediately feel appropriate to the place. Local gravel, the same colour as the stone, was used for cheapness and then in certain places we used more expensive materials, such as large reclaimed flags, to add weight to the landscaping.

The simplicity of the garden landscaping is its great virtue. Less is definitely more. No more than three different materials are used together: slate and stone in the Barn Garden; flags and stone on the terrace; and brick, wood and gravel in the Woodland Garden. We have minimized the accessories introduced into each area. Large simple pots add a sculptural element to the wild planting on the gravel; a wooden bench made from reclaimed oak planking adds focus to the walk through Tom's Wood. There is as little competition with the land as possible.

But the choice of materials has not always been easy. The access to the Woodland Garden lies close to the Victorian extension at the rear of the house. Although most of the property is stone-built, the extension at the back is of brick. Being so different to the rest of the property, it demanded a material for the access route that would blend with the walls without seeming out of place with the softness of the woodland planting.

After some searching, we found a local brick for the paths and walling. Although it looked right, it was not strictly appropriate for landscaping as it was porous and prone to cracking in frost. For paths you need an engineering brick or a brick that has been fired to a sufficiently high temperature not to weather when put in constant contact with moisture. We chose to risk it with the softer brick because the lichens it would attract would, in turn, make the garden look softer. The walls were roughly pointed and the paths laid on, and pointed with, sand to encourage moss. Although they have degraded, the paths are now soft and informal underfoot and look as if they have been there for ever.

With its south-facing ironstone walls and feeling of space and light, the front of the house demanded a different treatment. When we arrived, the area was no more than a small enclosure with a Victorian iron railing. The walls were made from red engineering brick and the dimensions were out of proportion seen against the stone walls of the house, inducing a feeling of claustrophobia. To get the proportions right, the terrace was reconfigured so that its depth matched the height of the house walls. A dry stone waller was contracted to make a wall from local stone to match and blend with the stone walls of the house. This wall would contain the rise of the terrace and allow views out across the landscape from within, but from outside it would give little indication that the front of the house had been gardened, thereby retaining its inherent simplicity.

Over the summer, the new wall rose slowly from the ground, and was a wonderful process to watch. It took six weeks to build, each stone being hand picked for its position from a heap of local stone that was delivered in a ten-ton truck. We had made the grave mistake

Local gravel blends with the stone walls and also the earth. It is cheap and flexible.

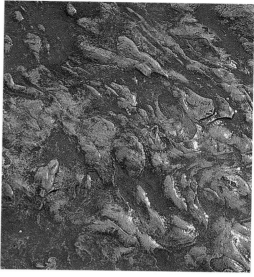

Some of the slabs on the terrace were laid upside down to reveal their texture.

Old cobbles in the Barn Garden were discovered under layer upon layer of ancient manure.

A path in the Barn Garden made from old slate reclaimed from the barn roof.

of dismantling an old wall along the drive that was crumbling, but which would have been better left in position. Although we did not salvage much from it, these pieces, added to the new wall, have, in time, helped to colonize it with lichens, encouraging it to blend in to the environment.

Some old flags for the terrace were found in a reclamation yard. We chose the largest we could handle so that each flag had a feeling of gravity to it. They are perfect for the terrace: strong and calming, and yet each has its own character. The stones were laid in a random pattern so that they merged with the beds and softened the edges. They were laid on sand so that the gaps between them could be taken over by softening plants and some were reversed so that their wonderful texture could be appreciated.

The way in which materials are used underfoot can influence the pace at which you move through a garden. Pattern will demand attention, so where you require free movement it is best avoided. Gravel is unchallenging to the eye and the grandeur and simplicity of the flags have a soundness about them that mean that you can pass over them with ease. But sometimes texture is useful underfoot as a means of slowing the pace. The cobbles that were found in the Barn Garden are a good example.

When we cleared the manure heap at the rear of the barn to make the garden there, the old cobbles we found were as good as buried treasure. Ancient and time worn, their undulations catch the light and their uneven texture adds to the sense of place. The surfaces here demand attention to slow the pace as we pick our way through the garden. The cobbles dictated the layout of the garden and are one of the reasons why it has always seemed 'right' there. A minor problem, however, was that they covered only a section of the area so the path was continued with slate that was broken up from re-roofing the barn. This gave us a link again to the building while the clack and crack of the tiles underfoot adds to the sensory experience.

TOOLS

The tools we use in the garden are basic but essential. There are none that stand by in the barn for a year without being used – tools can be hired if they are needed only infrequently. There are no gadgets and each implement is the best of its kind. This does not mean that all the tools are new – far from it; they are an idiosyncratic collection, some of which are worn and ancient but each is well balanced and comfortable to use. The tools are strong enough to be wielded without fear of breakage and the range allows us to choose the right tool for the right job.

The barrows are a good example. They are builders' barrows – cheap, easy to move and large enough to carry a good load. Constructed simply but well from metal, they are strong enough to move rocks, manure and soil, and well shaped so that they tip with ease. Their inflatable tyres need maintenance from time to time but allow you to move loads over

Sarah's portable tool bag with essential items: steel trowel, Felco secateurs and holster, fold-away saw and stout gloves.

rough ground without jolting. Every few years we have to go to the builders' merchants to replace one, but usually as a result of misuse or misadventure. One was inadvertantly backed over with a digger and another was used by the builders for cement mixing, becoming so encrusted that half the weight you were moving was fixed to the barrow.

The most frequently used hand-tools are the forks, spades and trowels. The best are of stainless steel, an investment up front, but a saving on energy long term. The heavy soil at Home Farm rarely sticks when using stainless steel so digging is made easier and jobs such as planting cleaner. We have two sizes of Spear and Jackson fork, which both have a moulded plastic handle: all-in-one handles are better than the composite ones, which can work loose and trap flesh in time. A tool should feel like an extension of your body and this particular fork is well designed. The angling of the handle and shaft is well orientated to the head and it is light but strong enough to feel comfortable. There is one standard and one border fork, which is smaller and ideal for weeding or for jobs that require a little more finesse.

There is no need for hand-forks as hand-trowels do just as well on a small scale. I have two favourites that are kept in the back of the car and travel everywhere. One is an old worn trowel with a wooden handle, which I have had for twenty years or so – it fits well in the palm and is warm to the touch. In the tool box I also have a new stainless steel trowel modelled on a Victorian design with a long, elegant blade that digs deep and is perfectly

My portable tool tray.
The coveted steel fork and
spade.

suited for whittling and targeting. The stainless steel is
preferable on this heavy soil, though I do not like to ignore
my old trowel.

Some tools are all the better for being old and well
worn and the best hoes are either hand-me-downs or those
picked up in sales. A fine, sharp and fairly small blade is
always the best. You can work between plants with a smaller
blade and, in a garden that is densely planted, precision
is vital. The handle should always be strong on a hoe and
long enough so that you can work with a straight back and
not have to bend. Whatever the tool it should always fit
the user for comfort.

We have a Dutch hoe and an onion hand-hoe. The
former is used regularly in the summer on dry windy days
so that the knocked-out weeds dry and die where they
land. The onion hoe is a beautiful little implement with
an arched head and a half-moon blade. It is used to draw
drills for sowing seed in the vegetable garden and for
intimate weeding where detail and precision is needed.

There are two rakes, a galvanized 'springbok', with
flexibility in the tines, and a flat-ended iron rake. The
former is used for clearing in the garden. The 'give' in its
tines is enough to be able to pass over plants without
dragging at them and yet hold the contour of the ground
it is passing over. The static head on the iron rake is used
at the end of winter to break up clods of earth that have
not been broken down by frost, and to level soil in the
vegetable garden. Both are essential.

Tools for hard graft include a strong pick for pulling
out rocks and roots, a 1kg (2lb) axe, a 500g (1lb) hand-
axe and a lump hammer for knocking in posts. We also
have an iron crowbar, which is useful for levering up stones
or slabs or for starting holes when staking.

The implements used for pruning are stored in a dry
place and kept oiled so that they perform well. As pruning
tools perform surgery they need, first and foremost, to
be sharp and, secondly, to be large enough to take on the
task so that a cut is never forced. We have the best secateurs
– there is no point in economizing here – produced by

Felco. Sarah prefers the swivel handle, which is kind on the hand on a long day's pruning, but I prefer the conventional Felco No.2 design. We avoid anvil secateurs as they crush the wood rather than cutting it with a scissor action. I also have an expensive but excellent pair of long-armed Felco pruners, which are useful when the wood is too large to cut with hand secateurs.

With the pruning equipment comes a fold-away hand saw, which is good for small limbs and fits neatly in the back pocket, plus a bow saw for larger wood. We will borrow a chain saw and accompanying safety mask, gloves and ear protectors as and when needed. The topiary is cut by hand with shears so that time can be taken to perfect the shape. The shears are produced by Spear and Jackson and have a flexible nylon handle that reduces repetitive strain injury by absorbing the jolts, and easily adjustable blades. All these tools are sharpened on a regular basis to keep them in good working order.

Steve brings with him a small electrical hedge cutter that is used to shear back the thyme after it has flowered and to cut the hedges and yew mounds. For safety, we have a contact breaker to go with it should the cable be cut, and we never use it in wet weather. The mowers we use are basic: a small petrol-driven rotary Hayter is used for cutting the little lawn in the top garden and for cutting the paths into the meadows. There is also a larger John Deere mini-tractor rotary mower for the larger expanses of grass. These are serviced annually and, when they are, they perform far better. There is a large four-stroke strimmer for keeping the bank in order (though a hover mower would be preferable) and an Allen scythe is hired in late summer to cut the meadows. This is a frightening instrument that has a bar of blades at the front like a floor-mounted hedge cutter. You have to cut the thatch at just the right moment as the blades will not cope if it is too wet.

There are other miscellaneous items integral to the successful running of the garden. Tarred string in large balls that will last a year is essential and, for the climbers, galvanized wire and vine eyes (decent grade wire and large vine eyes that will not bend under the weight of foliage). Steve brings old tarpaulins that have been rejected from the fire service and which are invaluable. They are used to insulate the compost heap, to put down on the gravel drive when the mulch is delivered, to cast over the Vegetable Garden to warm the soil and to keep it dry in the spring prior to sowing and, on occasion, to make a waterproof shelter to work under. There is a knapsack sprayer which was used occasionally for herbicide treatment when the bindweed and couchgrass was persistent and a smaller sprayer for emergency mildew treatment, though that is rarely used now as the mildew-prone roses have mostly been removed.

Last but not least are good gloves; everyone who comes to work in the garden tends to have their own. I have one leather pair for pruning thorny subjects and a lighter pair of welted rubber gloves that are produced by Sainsbury's. These are excellent, the welts give good grip and they are strong enough to last a winter. They are used when spreading fertiliser and for winter weeding when leather gloves are too cumbersome.

The bird table (above) is kept well stocked in winter. The bonfire (opposite) is an end-of-day job that is saved up for disposing of the pruning. The ash is spread around the roses as soon as it is cool.

NEW PROJECTS

The year never really comes to a close as the garden is always in a state of evolution.

It is not only the seasons that change the garden. As the gardeners here, we have to respond to change to retain the balance. The changes that we have made in the garden have each been different in their own way. Some have been designed with a very clear idea of what they were to become and others have come out of the need to redress a balance when a new mark was made on the land. It is an on-going process.

It is good that it has taken as long as it has to create the garden. We have needed time to get a feel for the place and to gain the confidence to move from one area to the next, while keeping an eye trained on the overall picture. One project will have a knock-on effect on the next and, despite the fact that we have now created a circuit around the whole garden that provides the link for all the separate chapters, the story is far from complete. We will need to rework it as plantings get out of balance and as we see things outside the garden that inform and inspire change – and change is never a bad thing.

In terms of planting, a new home will have to be found for the bergamot currently under the 'Scharlachglut' roses in the Barn Garden as the latter are now beginning to shade the bergamot. What has been in balance for five years will now need adjustment. The bergamot will be moved to a retentive position in sunshine to grow through the *Dahlia* 'Bishop of Llandaff' and the *Sanguisorba sanguinea* will be moved in under the roses, where its tall veil of dark thimbles will pick up the red. This will be a new and untested combination but one we hope will inject a new energy and interest into the Barn Garden.

The Thyme Garden is beginning to show its age now, five years after planting, despite the trim it is given after flowering. 'Porlock' has done infinitely better than the 'Silver Posie', which has shown itself to be the weaker of the two thymes and has started to die out and leave holes in the planting. This has not been seen as a disaster, more

as a chance to revitalize this area: there will be an annual task set up in mid-summer to take three or four hundred slip cuttings of the 'Porlock'. These will be lined out in a frame to be grown on in situ until they can be lifted and planted back into the holes the following spring. The planting will become plainer without the lightness of 'Silver Posie' but it can afford to now that the newly planted gravel area beyond it is becoming more interesting. The emphasis has changed and the balance shifted.

The Vegetable Garden has been an interesting development that has grown out of the desire to eat well. It started in the four beds by the kitchen but it has spread to become a productive hub and a garden very much in its own right. Its development has demanded that we incorporate it into the garden's narrative and also into the landscape, so that, in design terms, it will look and feel right where it is. As a result of its success, change has once again been prompted by the desire to introduce some glass under which early salad and the tomatoes can flourish. The tomatoes would yield better with more warmth (they are presently grown in the open) and the salad season could be extended.

There are certain parameters with a glasshouse. First and foremost, it needs to be in a position that is not overcast by trees. Ideally it should run east/west to maximize light and be close to the house so that it will be easy to access for regular maintenance. It will

need a supply of water on hand and paths leading to and from it. It will also need to be big enough to grow a range of plants and still allow freedom of movement. We also need to ensure that it will fit in visually so ideally it will be made from cedar.

Its imminent arrival has already prompted a ring of changes. The raspberries have been moved from the bank, using the summer-fruiting plants in a line to screen the compost heap and the autumn-fruiting plants down near the salad beds to replace the old defunct frames there. These have been dismantled and will need to be replaced near the new glasshouse. They will face due south if they run along the front of the proposed glasshouse so will need shading in summer, but this seems to be a good place for them.

Moving the raspberries has prompted us to think about constructing a fruit cage, which will mean extending the stock beds that lie beyond the barn walls. A new fruit area would include white and redcurrants – one bush of each 2m (6ft) apart – gooseberries and strawberries. The raspberries will most probably move again to join them and then we will have to start thinking about adding to the young orchard which was moved when the pond was excavated. These are just some of the immediate tasks that present themselves and offer us momentum. Without change the garden would be without its essential spark – and, no doubt, so would we.

INDEX

AUTHOR'S ACKNOWLEDGEMENTS

Firstly, I have to thank all those people who have inspired me as a gardener. Particular thanks go to Mum and Dad for your constant interest and enthusiasm, and to Geraldine and the late Frances Pumphrey.

There are many people who have contributed to the garden at Home Farm over time. Thanks go to Jane for your contribution in the early days. Thanks also to Roddy for your artfully laid terrace and to Simon for your exchange of labour and for helping me to build the first garden in Barnes. There are many people who have contributed with their craftsmanship. Particular thanks go to Michael, the stone-waller, both for showing us that each stone has its own place and for creating a wall that gives pleasure every time it is seen.

Thanks go, too, to all the people who work at Home Farm today. Steve, we could not do without your vigilance and commitment, and Sarah, your constant reminder that the garden is just part of a greater thing. Thanks, too, to Bernard for keeping the lawn in order. Nikki Browne, your images capture the fleeting beauty of the place, and thank you, Huw, for your comprehension and picture selection, and for the beautiful short film that inspired the idea of recording the garden over a year.

We would also like to thank the BBC and all those involved in the process of making and crafting the series. Severn Trent Water were extremely generous in their sponsorship of the wildlife pond and English Nature also, with their financial contribution to the wild-flower meadow. Thanks go to Ebury for taking on the challenge of publishing something so heart-felt. And thank you to David Mossman for letting us use the old photographs of Home Farm on pages 12–15.

If it were not for the nurturing environment that Frances has created at Home Farm, none of these things would have been possible. It is a good place that is made all the better for your generosity.

First published in Great Britain in 2001 • 1 3 5 7 9 10 8 6 4 2 • Text © Dan Pearson 2001 • Photography © Nicola Browne 2001 • Dan Pearson has asserted his right to be identified as the author of this work under the Copyright, Designs and Patents Act 1988. • All rights reserved. No part of this publication may be reproduced, stored in a retrieval system, or transmitted in any form or by any means, electronic, mechanical, photocopying, recording or otherwise without the prior permission of the copyright owners. • "By arrangement with the BBC • The BBC logo is a trade mark of the British Broadcasting Corporation and is used under licence." • BBC logo © 1996 • First published by Ebury Press • Random House, 20 Vauxhall Bridge Road, London SW1V 2SA • Random House Australia (Pty) Limited, 20 Alfred Street, Milsons Point, Sydney, New South Wales 2061, Australia • Random House New Zealand Limited, 18 Poland Road, Glenfield, Auckland 10, New Zealand • Random House South Africa (Pty) Limited, Endulini, 5A Jubilee Road, Parktown 2193, South Africa • The Random House Group Limited Reg. No. 954009 • www.randomhouse.co.uk • A CIP catalogue record for this book is available from the British Library. • Editors: Sharon Amos, Susan Berry • Designer: The Senate • Picture editor: Huw Morgan • ISBN 0 09 187032 1 • Papers used by Ebury Press are natural, recyclable products made from wood grown in sustainable forests. • Printed and bound in France by Imprimerie Pollina.